CAPTAIN MATTHEW TURNER

CAPTAIN MATTHEW TURNER

WORLD-CLASS SHIPBUILDER

H. ALLAN GANDY

Alive Book Publishing

Captain Matthew Turner
World-Class Shipbuilder
Copyright © 2024 by H. Allan Gandy

All rights reserved. No part of this book may be reproduced or transmitted in any form or by any means without written permission from the publisher and author.

Additional copies may be ordered from the publisher for educational, business, promotional or premium use. For information, contact ALIVE Book Publishing at: alivebookpublishing.com, or call (925) 837-7303.

Cover photo of Matthew Turner: Museum of History Benicia
Back cover photo: Museum of History Benicia
with photo enhancement by Wahid Ahad
About the Author photo by Susan Gandy

ISBN 13
978-1-63132-243-3

Library of Congress Control Number: 2024924105
Library of Congress Cataloging-in-Publication Data is available upon request.

First Edition

Published in the United States of America by ALIVE Book Publishing and ALIVE Publishing Group, imprints of Advanced Publishing LLC
3200 A Danville Blvd., Suite 204, Alamo, California 94507
alivebookpublishing.com

PRINTED IN THE UNITED STATES OF AMERICA

10 9 8 7 6 5 4 3 2 1

Acknowledgments

Many thanks to Museum of History Benicia research associate Bob Kvasnicka for helping provide research of historical details on Matthew Turner's ships and events. I am also grateful to my colleagues at the museum for their help and support: James E. Lessenger, researcher and author, for donating his time for editorial suggestions, and archives curator Beverly Phelan. And a special thanks to Nathaniel Howe, Executive Director, Puget Sound Maritime Historical Society, for helping identify Matthew Turners vessels from the 1880's and 1890's.

Thanks to researchers who in the past have dedicated their time to gathering information about Matthew Turner's life and sailing vessels:

- Gina Bardi – Librarian at the San Francisco Maritime National Historical Library, National Park Service, for helping with access to the largest collection of Matthew Turner historical documents and images.
- Dr. John L Lyman – Professor of Marine Science at the University of North Carolina, who would study and write about maritime history. He published his own periodicals, *Log Chips, Marine Digest,* and *Nautical Research Journal* from 1932 to 1978.
- Don K. Oliver – Researcher who transcribed some of the original diary of Matthew Turner in the 1960s and 1970s, worked with the Matthew Turner Foundation on research.
- Murray Chapman Hunt and the Hunt family – Decedents of the Chapman family who donated much of their collection of Matthew Turner photographs to the Museum of History Benicia.
- Thomas J. Le Vell – Director of the Matthew Turner Foundation 1990s, worked on Turner's biography and attempted to raise money to build a replica of Turner's *Geneva*. The foundation collapsed in 2006 when Le Vell died.
- May Colling – Researcher, publisher of two compilations about the Finnish in her neighborhood via the Ashtabula County Genealogical Society, and extensive research on Matthew Turner from the 1970s to 1990s.

To my son Ryan, the tall ship in my heart

Contents

Introduction	13
Chapter One: Matthew Turner's Early Days	15
Chapter Two: Matthew Turner's Journey to California	23
Chapter Three: Matthew Turner in California Gold Country	27
Chapter Four: The Pacific Journeys of the Young Matthew Turner	31
Chapter Five: Matthew Turner's Cod Fishing Journeys	43
Chapter Six: The Brigantine *Nautilus*	49
Chapter Seven: Matthew Turner's Shipyard in San Francisco	61
Chapter Eight: Matthew Turner Shipyard Moves to Benicia	77
Chapter Nine: The Brigantine *Galilee*	91
Chapter Ten: Matthew Turner's Later Years	107
Chapter Eleven: The Shipyard is Sold to James Robertson	123
Chapter Twelve: Tales of Matthew Turner's Ships	131
Chapter Thirteen: The *Matthew Turner* Tall Ship	159
Appendix A: List of ships designed and built by Matthew Turner	161
Appendix B: Sailing Records of Matthew Turner Ships	181
Appendix C: Known Fates of Matthew Turner Ships	183
Appendix D: Ship Types of the 19th Century	189
Appendix E: Glossary of Nautical Terminology	191

Preface

Matthew Turner was a well-known shipbuilder in Benicia and San Francisco. When I visit his Benicia shipyard site, which was in operation from 1883 to 1904, I enjoy imagining tall ships setting sail onto the Carquinez Strait on their way to San Francisco. Since no complete biography of Matthew Turner could be found, I was inspired to research his life and ships and compile all accounts into this book.

The Matthew Turner Foundation was established in the early 1970s with the goal of retrieving and publishing information about the renowned shipbuilder. Don K. Oliver, a researcher, had access to Turner's 1850 to 1853 diary, and he interpreted Turner's life during those years. Information about Turner's later years was gathered from newspaper articles detailing vessel launches, ship movements in and out of San Francisco, ship cargos, and periodic personal information about Turner. Oliver wrote several hundred pages of material that aligned with Turner's timeline, with the intention of releasing them as a biography book. Oliver's accounts included assumptions about Turner's thoughts and actions, and even created dialogues and conversations. Unfortunately, the Matthew Turner Foundation ceased to exist in the late 1990s following the passing of Oliver and researcher Thomas J. Le Vell in 2006.

This book contains some of Oliver's compelling stories about Matthew Turner's actions and discussions, which portray Turner's world of ships and adventures. Turner was always on the go, creating business prospects while pursuing his passion for sailing. While some of the dialogue is quoted as Turner's words, it is only an estimation of what may have transpired. Nevertheless, it provides an internal look into what Turner may have been experiencing.

Before Richard Rundle passed away, Turner promised to take care of Ashbeline and her children. In 1878, he married Ashbeline Rundle, and their bond lasted 28 years. They enjoyed entertaining by hosting yacht club parties and ship launch celebrations. Turner deeply cared for Ashbeline, her children, and especially their granddaughter Eva. He was a devoted husband, father, and grandfather figure.

The Turner shipyards were well equipped with materials, equipment, and labor, allowing them to quickly fulfill orders for small vessels. Since many of these boats did not require a certificate of registration, they were not included in Turner's count of ships built. The Daily Alta California, which originated from the first newspaper published in San Francisco, Samuel Brannan's California Star, was first published on January 9, 1847. Many accounts of Matthew Turner and his ships in this book come from newspapers.

Introduction

Figure 1: Captain Matthew Turner.
Source: Museum of History Benicia.

Matthew Turner was an accomplished American sea captain, shipbuilder, and ship designer who is credited with constructing a total of 265 vessels. Out of these, 184 were built in his shipyard located in Benicia, California. His remarkable contributions to the shipbuilding industry on the Pacific Coast have earned him the reputation of being the grandfather of big-time wooden shipbuilding in the region. He holds the distinction of being the most prolific builder of sailing vessels in the United States.

Matthew Turner was known for building unique sailing vessels along the Pacific Coast. In the early 19th century, conventional shipbuilding design dictated that seagoing vessels needed a broad beam bow to prevent flipping over due to enormous ocean waves. However, Turner challenged this idea and constructed ships that were long and sharp forward, with a lean and full design on the waterline aft. Many people doubted his idea, claiming that it would make the ship dive into the water and always be wet. But the design features actually helped Turner's ships outperform all other sailing ships of the era. While sailing in the Pacific Ocean, Turner developed the Bermuda sail, which was a triangular sail that was much more adapted to the weather in the Pacific. Additionally, Turner built some of the fastest racing yachts in the world, as proven during the famous races sponsored by the San Francisco Yacht Club, of which Turner was a charter member.

The Pacific Coast schooners and barkentines were primarily designed to transport a specific type of cargo, which was redwood and fir lumber. Their main goal was to carry a massive load, mostly on the deck, and unload it as quickly as possible. If there was no return freight available, they would sail back to the mill port empty. But there were other types of trade ships which a large number were purchased by owners in the South Pacific islands that carried passengers, mail, and fresh fruit. There were also ships for the sugar industry that sailed the San Francisco to Hawaii trade route. In the Pacific north, there was the cod fish industry.

In the windy San Francisco Bay, there were boats called "scow schooners". These boats had a broad, shallow draft, were square-ended, and had a moderate two-masted schooner rig. They were used to transport goods that would now be transported by the trucking industry. The San Francisco Bay was also a popular location for yacht clubs that hosted races.

Matthew Turner was highly skilled in marine architecture and ship design. However, with the advent of steam power and steel hulls, the use of wooden hulls and canvas sails became obsolete by the turn of the century. As a result, his shipyard was closed down in 1904. Nevertheless, he continues to be remembered for his exceptional work in the field.

Chapter One
Matthew Turner's Early Days

Matthew Turner's story begins in Geneva, Ashtabula County, Ohio. His parents were George and Emily Atkins Turner. George, born in Montville, Connecticut on August 12, 1794, came to the Connecticut Western Reserve (now eastern Ohio) in 1821. He settled in Jefferson, the seat of the newly erected Ashtabula County. At the age of 27, George was a man of charming manners, and personal appearance and had a talent for music, drawing, and penmanship.[1]

His wife, Emily Atkins, was born in Monroe, Ohio on December 16, 1804. They were married on January 20, 1822. They had four girls (Sarah, Stella, Ada, and Phedora) and two boys (Horatio and Matthew).

George Turner acquired a farm from his father-in-law located on both sides of Indian Creek at Geneva, near the shore of Lake Erie. Turner was a skilled mechanic and an inventive man. He made use of the creek to irrigate his farm. In 1825, he constructed a dam to create a deep pond and established the first sawmill in this part of Ohio. As settlers in Ohio were moving from log cabins to proper homes built with lumber, Turner's sawmill served this growing market.[2] The lumber produced by his mill was not only used for building homes but also for shipbuilding. Many of the old homes of Geneva-on-the-Lake and eastern Geneva Township were built with lumber sawed at Turner's mill.

Figure 2: Map of Ashtabula County showing Indian Creek and Geneva (arrow) along Lake Erie where the Turners lived.
Source: William Sumner, Nelson Township, Portage County, Ohio, 1826.

Figure 3: Scene of Indian Creek where it flows into Lake Erie, circa 1900. George Turner's sawmill was near this location.
Source: Postcard, L.P. Jones, Geneva, Ohio.

In 1831, George Turner became a Coronel in the state militia as stated in a letter from the governor of Ohio.[3]

In the name and by the authority of the State of Ohio, Duncan McArthur, Governor, and Commander in Chief of said state:

To George Turner, Greetings:
You have been duly elected Coronel of the Third Regiment, Third Brigade, Ninth Regiment in the militia of this state.
Signed:
Duncan McArthur, Governor
M. H. Kirby, Secretary of State

Colonel Turner wore his elaborate uniform, with epaulets and cocked hat, with sword and sash, on general training days, though he never saw any duty. He retained the title for the remainder of his years as the state militias were merged into the National Guard in 1916.

In the fall of 1838, Colonel Turner and a partner, Thomas Makepeace Fitch, began constructing a sloop, the *Geneva*, near the sawmill. The simple boat had a burden of just 30 tons, but launching it proved to be a challenge. When spring 1839 arrived, the little boat was moved into the stream with teams of oxen to take advantage of a burst of high water from heavy rain. To provide sufficient draft to launch the sloop, floodgates on the mill dam upstream were opened providing additional depth. When the vessel reached the bridge across the creek, with the aid of several neighbors and many oxen, it was drawn to deeper water at the mouth of the creek. Once it was in deeper waters, she was fitted with a mast and sail and on her way into Lake Erie.[4] Martin Watrous of Ashtabula, Ohio, purchased the sloop *Geneva* and ran it in the limestone trade between Ashtabula and the western Lake Erie islands. Matthew and Horatio were growing into manhood and each was learning the art of seamanship on the Great Lakes, and looking forward to something more than the command of a sloop.[5]

In 1845, George Turner built a new sawmill in a more accessible location, after the success of his first shipbuilding venture. The old dam was strengthened and raised, and a race was built from the pond to the mill, along with new machinery. The carriage of the new mill was large enough to handle logs 60 feet in length.[6] These improvements allowed for the production of various types of wood and vessel materials, such as planking and decking.

In 1846, George Turner hired James Lockwood of Geneva to build a second ship, the *Philena Mills*.

James Mills and Eliakim Roberts were the investors. They built the ship from 1846 to 1847 using oak harvested from the nearby Saybrook Township. No local lumber was deemed suitable for its masts, so the lumber for that was brought using oxen from Sorrel Hill, Pennsylvania, about 40 miles away. The *Philena Mills* was 100 feet long, rated at 270 tons, and was considered one of the finest sailing ships of its time on the Great Lakes.[7]

Matthew was born June 17, 1825 in Geneva. As a young child, he was surrounded by ships and shipbuilding activity. Matthew was just 16 when his 36-year-old mother Emily and an infant daughter passed away during childbirth on March 3, 1841.[8] His father George remarried later that year in October to Lucretia Blakeslee. They had a son together, George E., born in 1843.

Turner's older brother, Horatio Nelson Turner, was born in June 1823. In the 1840s, Horatio captained the *Philena Mills* on Lake Erie for his father's business.

Horatio married Arsinoe Morrison on July 4, 1851, in Warrick, Indiana. They lived in Chicago for six years before Arsinoe died on January 11, 1858. They had two children, (Eva Arsinoe Turner born 1853, and Louis Horatio Turner born 1856).

Mary Atkins, Emily Turner's younger sister, was born in Jefferson, Ohio, in 1819 and was an 1845 graduate of Oberlin College. She came to California via Panama in 1853 and moved to Benicia in 1854. At the request of the Trustees of the Benicia Young Ladies' Seminary, she became principal and proprietor in 1854. Later in 1855 she paid $2,495 for the buildings and property and became the owner as well. In 1865 Atkins sold the seminary to Susan and Cyrus Mills for $5,000, who moved the seminary in 1871 to Oakland, and was renamed as Mills College. Mary married Major John C. Lynch, attorney for many years, in 1869, and both lived in Benicia. Mary was Matthew's aunt.

At the age of 18, Matthew Turner acquired his master mariner certificate, which allowed him to captain vessels, and he spent some time in command of various vessels. He became an apprentice in the shipbuilding industry along the Great Lakes and paid close attention to the construction of the *Geneva* and the *Philena Mills*. He designed a ship of his own at the age of 22. He revealed his design to his father, and George was so impressed with the concept that he swept his arm past the long rows of lumber sawed at his mill and said, "Son, there is the lumber, so go ahead and build her."[9] Matthew then built and launched the *George R. Roberts* schooner in 1848, named in honor of one of George's business associates. The vessel was broad of beam and well suited for the lumber trade. The mast this time was pine that came from the swamps of Saybrook, five miles east of Geneva.

Under the capable command of Matthew Turner, the *George R. Roberts* proved herself to be one of the fastest and safest sailing ships on the Great Lakes. Matthew ended his maiden sailing season triumphantly, with his marriage to Amanda Jackson on September 16, 1848. It was love at first sight. Matthew and Amanda were married at her home in Richland County, about 125 miles from Geneva. As to how they met when such great distance separated their homes is unknown. Amanda was soft-spoken, gentle-mannered, brown-eyed, and very lovely. Their wedded bliss was short-lived as almost before they could become adjusted to their life together, she contracted a fever and died.[10]

The grief that Matthew Turner must have been unbearable. To deal with his grief, he left Geneva on December 6, 1848, aboard the *George R. Roberts* and headed out on Great Lakes and busied himself with lumber runs. When Turner came up missing at the end of the season, his family was so worried about his disappearance that his father placed ads in the papers along the Great Lakes seeking information about his son.[11] The following notice appeared in an Ashtabula County newspaper in December 1848.[12]

> $500 Reward — Mysterious Disappearance:
>
> Captain Matthew Turner of the schooner *G.R. Roberts* left the city of Geneva, Ashtabula County, on the 6th of December last.
>
> On the following day, his name was registered upon the book at the Commercial Hotel in Detroit, since which, no tidings of him have been received. Although inquiry and search has been unremitted, no trace of Captain Turner has been discovered.
>
> He is known to have with him a considerable sum of money, and also the books of the schooner, and fears are entertained that he might have met with violent death.
>
> His father and brother, Colonel George and Captain H. N. Turner offer a reward of five hundred dollars for the discovery and arrest of the perpetrators of the deed, and proportionately for any intelligence which may lead to a knowledge of the fate of the son and brother. Detroit, Cleveland and Buffalo papers will confer a favor upon his distressed family and friends by publishing this notice, and communications relating to it may be addressed to this office, or Captain H. N. Turner of this city.

Figure 4: Newspaper article regarding Matthew Turner's disappearance. Source: *Ashtabula Sentinel*, December 1848.

The newspaper notice brought no further whereabouts of Matthew to his family. He was on Lake Michigan making money hauling timber to Chicago. Matthew eventually returned home, in his own timing, unaware of the concern he had caused his family.

President James K. Polk announced the discovery of gold in California in his State of the Union address on December 5, 1848. "Accounts of the abundance of gold are of such an extraordinary character as would scarcely command belief," he said. Hearing about the Gold Rush, Matthew told his father "Papa, I think I would like to go out to California and see the goldfields. I have done all I can here, and have a feeling to see California." His father replied "Matt, you go to California. I think it will be good for you. Write us when you can."[13]

Matthew selected his attire and brought his Hawkin rifle, along with money earned from the lumber trade on Lake Erie, for his journey to California. He boarded a lake schooner that carried lumber through the narrows into Lake St. Clair, then into Lake Huron, through the Mackinac Strait into Lake Michigan, and down to Chicago. The schooner may have been the *George R. Roberts* as she was sold in December 1849, in Muskegon to A. R. H. Atkins.[14] The *George R. Roberts*

was based out of Chicago and changed owners ten more times between 1850 and 1878.[15]

He spent a week with his brother who lived in Chicago. On December 7, 1849, he boarded a flatboat and made his way down the Illinois River 300 miles to Portage Des Sioux, where he took passage on a Mississippi riverboat to New Orleans.[16]

Turner welcomed the new passengers at each stopping point down the river. At the stop in St. Louis, Turner met a man named Spike Moyes. Moyes had traveled down the Missouri River from the Dakota territory. Turner had never seen a man like Moyes before. He wore buckskins and carried no luggage, but he handled his rifle, also a Hawkin, as if it were made of gold. Moyes had the face of a mountain man, possibly a native American. He paid no attention to the men, only to their gear. Moyes asked, "This your rifle?" Turner replied, "It's the best rifle I own, and I wouldn't go to California without it." Moyes was impressed and befriended Turner.[17]

Turner and Moyes traveled to New Orleans, where they enjoyed exploring the city for a week. As migrants heading to California, they had two sea routes to choose from: crossing the Panama isthmus or rounding the horn. For safety reasons, they joined a group of fellow travelers and chartered a schooner to take them to Chagres, located on the Caribbean side of the Isthmus of Panama.

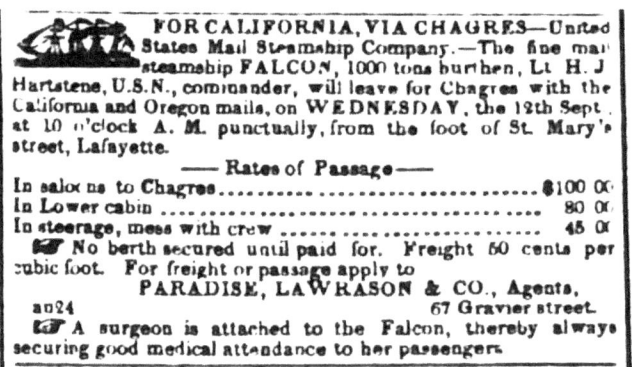

Figure 5: 1850 advertisement for U.S. Mail Steamship Company passage on the steamship *Falcon* to Chagres.
Source: *The Daily Delta*, New Orleans, March 16, 1850.

They departed the schooner at Chagres River and went ashore on a sandy beach. Their journey had begun, with no turning back. After gathering all available boats and canoes, the group made arrangements with the locals to transport them 30 miles up the Chagres River to Pelenkina. As they started their journey through the hot tropical jungle, they kept the boats together. The group was amazed by the beautifully colored birds that filled the trees of the dense forest, and the constant chatter attracted the monkeys, who joined in protest against the intrusion of their habitat. The men sat with their rifles across their knees, taking turns rowing while occasionally relieving the natives. After traveling 10 miles, they stopped at Gatún to rest and eat before continuing their journey. At night, the boats were brought together, and the men took turns guarding them throughout the night. On the second day, the palm trees stretched their fronds across the narrows, and banana trees were occasionally seen. By the time they reached Pelenkina at noon, every boat had a stock of fruit with them. They paid the natives and found a lodging house where they spent the night.[18]

On their journey, they had to climb a long and difficult trail from Pelenkina to Cruses, which was 20 miles away. The path they took was an ancient one that had once been paved with boulders. They covered half of the distance and then set up camp for the night. The air was cooler that night, and the men were exhausted. The following day, they continued their journey towards Cruses, which was 25 miles away from their previous campsite. In the late afternoon, they crossed the Continental Divide and set up camp for the night. The next morning, they resumed their journey and by the end of the day, they arrived in Panama City. They had spent five days crossing the isthmus, covering a distance of 85 miles.[19]

Chapter Two
Matthew Turner's Journey to California

Matthew Turner was on his way to California. In Panama City, Turner and Moyes boarded the *Marianna* on March 11, 1850. The *Marianna* was a fast clipper packet, under the command of Captain Dering, and famous for making the trip around the Horn from New York to San Francisco in 123 days. She had superior cabin and steerage accommodations, and a well-ventilated saloon, having four patent ventilators on either side. She also had four stern windows and three hatchways, with wind tails (wind direction indicators). She was furnished throughout with new mattresses, pillows, and clean sheets. She was supplied with the best provisions of vegetables and fruits, and 15,000 gallons of fresh spring water.[20]

Turner kept a diary during this trip[21] and the first entry was ten days into the voyage. Some of the passengers on the vessel were very sick from the isthmus crossing.

> *On March 21, 1850: I am off to California, and now far away over the deep blue sea from all the friends and home of my childhood. Ten days has the good ship Marianna glided over the water with a fair wind and stunsails set, many days and many months must pass away before we arrive at the destined port of San Francisco, the Capitol of the new El Dorado.*
>
> *Sunday, March 24, 1850: Winds N NE. Blowing soft and mild as a summer breeze. We are in the prescribed limits of those eternal winds, the trades, which have blown from the beginning of time and must continue on their westerly course to all Eternity.*
>
> *Thursday, March 28, 1850: Calm. Calm eternal calm. Fourteen days since we left from which we are about nine hundred miles distant. 8 p,m. one of the passengers (a darkey) died,*
>
> *Friday, March 29, 1850: Buried the dead at eight bell a.m. One of the passengers read the ceremony. "We commit this body to the deep" said he, and the plank was inclined and the body was launched into the sea.*

Matthew studied the steadiness of the trade winds that always intrigued him when he read about them in his nautical books. He would observe ships that would sail past in voyages up or down the coast. Most of his entries contained wind conditions and latitude and longitude positions.

Sunday, March 31, 1850: This is the beginning of another week, and the end of March. That month usually so boisterous and stormy has been beautifully pleasant.

Monday, April 1st, "Fools Day." A packet hove in site which proved to be a fore-and-aft schooner wearing a U. States flag and apparently on her way to San Francisco.

Matthew spent much of his time on the journey talking to the crew and asking questions about the operation of the ship, the weather, and the currents. He was paying attention to navigation, watched the crew as they used the sextant, chronometer, and chip log, and the formulae for plotting their course. On and off, Matthew felt sick, having attacks of ague, a malarial fever marked by chills and sweating. He most likely contracted malaria crossing the isthmus.

Monday, April 8, 1850: Made Clipperton Rock. Lat 10 Long 109. A barren rock surrounded by a shoal of sand and rock of about three miles in length. (Clipperton Rock, 695 miles southwest of Mexico, is the only coral atoll in the tropical eastern Pacific.)

Friday, April 12, 1850. Wind N NE. Lat 13.51 north, Long 117.30 west. Employed during the last watch caulking decks, repairing ship's long boat, also made a kind of guitar. With this instrument, a triangle fiddle in form, and two or three bottles with their bottom knocked out for horns, some of the passengers gave a concert for the edification of the rest.

Sunday, April 14, 1850: Wind N.E. blowing fresh. Great excitement on board last night. A meeting was held and Officers were nominated for Governor of California. After the brandy and beer were circulated, electioneering ran high. Speeches were made, songs sung, and the candidates were carried about on the shoulders of their advocates with patriotic enthusiasm. During the excitement the band repeatedly serenaded the aspirants to office, performing some of their best pieces which received with uproaring laughter. At length the excitement wore off and the evenings performance ended with music and dancing. Wind N.E. blowing fresh. Lat 17.57 Long 120.44.

Tuesday, April 23, 1850: Winds light and variable. Weather very pleasant. Had a grand spree last night. Got tighter than I ever was before. Moyes drunk as a boiled owl. Lat 35.26 Long 132. (The reference to Moyes is Spike Moyes whom Turner met in St. Louis).[22]

Wednesday, April 24, 1850: Winds light and variable between north and east. Lat 36.30 Long 131.15. One of my shipmates taken sick, brought on by a spree on the night of the 23rd. Sighted a brig and an English barque, apparently bound for San Francisco.

Thursday, April 25, 1850: Winds N. NE. blowing fresh in the afternoon with fog and drizzling rain. Had an attack of ague and fever, Lat 38.05 Long 133,30.

Tuesday, April 30, 1850: Winds N.E. Blowing fresh. Ague and fever have reduced me considerably. Lat 40.36 Long132.06. A man in the steerage has been very sick with dysentery and is now considered very dangerous. He is from Boston, and is an agent for some merchant.

Wednesday, May 1, 1850: Made out land northward of San Francisco about 3:00 PM, Lat. 38.36 Long 123.30. Making preparations to disembark on the morrow as all expect to arrive sometime tomorrow at the celebrated city of San Francisco.

Thursday, May 2, 1850: Lay to this morning to daylight. We then saw the Padrone Islands (Farallones) 21 miles from the San Francisco Bay. Filled the main topsail and stood in for the harbor. Took a pilot and proceeded, arriving at San Francisco about 1 p.m. Lowered a boat and went ashore. Found things much as I expected. Saw some acquaintances from Chicago.

Due to the number of ships clustered at the San Francisco harbor, the *Marianna* dropped anchor off a sandy beach beyond Black Point, near the Presidio. Matthew Turner had arrived! The 48-day journey from Panama had come to an end.[23]

Spike Moyes and Turner lowered a boat from the *Marianna* and rowed it ashore. Downtown San Francisco was a three-mile walk following a trail up a hill and over sand dunes and fields of grass. From the top, they could see the *Marianna*. Down on the flats were poorly constructed shacks used by immigrants on the way to the goldfields. The bay was a big body of water with three prominent islands offshore: Angel Island, Bird Island (Alcatraz), and Goat Island (Yerba Buena). They could see hundreds of ships anchored along San Francisco's water edge.

Figure 6: Ships were abandoned in San Francisco as crews headed for the gold fields, 1850.
Source: National Geographic.

In San Francisco, Turner and Moyes had one thought in mind. They were going to find a saloon and have a howling good time.[24] After their daily outings, they spent each night back on the *Marianna*. They met a man selling a small boat rigged with sails, and Turner liked the boat and bought her. He would use the boat to navigate east toward the goldfields. After spending seven days in San Francisco, Turner and Moyes were ready to head to the mountains.

Chapter Three
Matthew Turner in California Gold Country

On May 9, 1850, Matthew Turner and Spike Moyse said goodbye to the *Marianna* and traveled north on their small boat through San Pablo Bay into the Carquinez Strait. They stopped along shore at Benicia during the evening and set up their tent for the night. Turner mentioned the trip in his diary:

> *Thursday, May 9, 1850: Went onshore and bought some necessities. Went aboard and loaded our boat, and started bidding good by to the ship Marianna and her gentlemanly officers. Had a very windy day and rough sea. Arrived at Benicia about dark. Pitched our tent on the bank, but the tide rose and wet us out. So we took to the boat for the rest of the night,*

The next morning, they traveled east to Stockton, the hub of business and transportation to the southern mines. Upon reaching Stockton, they purchased mining equipment and exchanged their boat for a horse. They then headed towards the North Fork of the Calaveras River and arrived there by morning. Continuing their journey, they traveled 25 miles to another spot along the Calaveras River, where they discovered an abundance of gold diggings. On May 17, Turner found his first gold, nearly 3 dollars worth, after digging for three hours.

Turner continued to make entries in his diary documenting his daily gold finds. Like most gold prospectors, Turner kept on the move searching new creeks and rivers, buying claims, and digging tools. Turner usually rested on Sundays "keeping the Sabbath, it being the Lords command."

Turner turned 25 years of age on June 17. His back was aching and nothing special was written in his diary.

> *Monday, June 17, 1850: Started for home and arrived at 3 P. M., a distance of 30 miles. Moyes brought with him Brownsfield B. Mason, from the western states.*

Later that month on June 24, he met his friend Dr. Ben Crocker and prospected for gold at San Antonio Creek camp, 11 miles east of Murphys in Calaveras County, California.

On July 14, Turner departed for Murphys Diggings about 20 miles away. On July 25, he bought two claims for $50 and dug $80 (4 ounces of gold). He learned that Murphys was not a safe area as his diary entry reflects:

> *Wednesday, August 14, 1850. I am now in the company of the most miserable drunken Devils that ever existed. If I get through them peacably t'will be a wonder. One of them has often threatened to whip me, yet he has never attempted it, for he knows very well that he is not able to do it. Company dangerous.*

Although Turner had success at Murphys Diggings, he returned to San Antonio Creek where he had his best success in September digging for $1,259.75 in gold, about 61 ounces. Here is a five-day stretch of his diary entries:

> *Tuesday, September 10, 1850: Diggings weatherbound. Very cloudy with probable rain. Dug $10.*
> *Wednesday, September 11, 1850: Dug $148. Quite cold and cloudy.*
> *Thursday, September 12, 1850: Dug $156 and rested. Cold and cloudy.*
> *Friday. September 13, 1850: Dug $18. Weather continuing cold.*
> *Saturday, September 14, 1850: Cold and cloudy. Dug $58.*

Feeling homesick, Moyes left for San Francisco on September 30. October was a good month for Turner as he dug $407.50 in gold (19 ½ ounces).

On November 15, Turner realized that a tent would not be suitable for the winter, and began building a wooden frame house. On November 17, Moyes returned and brought Turner letters from his brother Horatio and his sister Sarah. Turner and Moyes finished building the house on November 22. However, the chimney initially smoked them out, and it had to be rebuilt several times to achieve the proper draft. Finally, the house was ready to help them stay dry throughout the Sierra Nevada winter.

Throughout Turner's time in the goldfields, he suffered from back pain and sore and painful eyes. The symptoms of scurvy were well known to the miners, but the cure was not known. Turner knew that they lacked citrus fruit, but were not able to procure any.

During his first year, 8 months in the gold fields, Turner was very prosperous. He documented in his diary digging $3,104 in gold (150 ounces).

As the new year began in 1851, Turner did not make any entries in his diary. He continued to prospect the gold in Calaveras and Tuolumne counties. He met

Figure 7: Matthew Turner using a sluice rocker box in San Antonio Creek camp near Murphys in the search for gold, 1850. His friend Dr. Ben Crocker is behind, using a gold pan. Source: The Hunt Family.

an Englishman named Richard Thomas Rundle, who like Turner was a sea captain.[25] From 1852 to 1853, Turner and Rundle were partners in a small gold mining operation at Big Oak Flat, 25 miles west of Yosemite Valley. Turner and Rundle would remain close friends and business partners throughout their lives. Spike Moyes parted ways during this time, but his destination was unknown.

Turner continued to do well in the gold country. Although the exact amount was unknown, he must have earned over $10,000 during his adventure. Matthew Turner had planned to stay three years in the goldfields, and after the severe winter of 1852-1853, he was ready to return to San Francisco in the summer.

Figure 8: The gold mine in Big Oak Flat, Tuolumne County, where Matthew Turner and Richard Rundle were partners from 1852 to 1853. Source: The Hunt Family.

Chapter Four
The Pacific Journeys of the Young Matthew Turner

Matthew Turner did well in the gold fields and remained until August 14, 1853, after which he and Richard Rundle returned to San Francisco several days later with a "heavy load" of gold. Turner and Rundle took their gold to Wells Fargo where it was weighed and the dollar amount tallied. They both took a $500 draft as they intended to have a good time before they ventured into a serious business enterprise.[26]

San Francisco had changed significantly in three years. The common shacks were replaced by multistory buildings and the city was pushing over the hills in a westerly direction. Some of the streets were paved with cobblestone. The downtown area was pulsing with activity. Turner stopped by a photography business and had his picture taken so he could send it back to his father in Ohio.

Figure 9: Matthew Turner, 1853, age 28.
Source: The Hunt Family.

The Gold Rush had brought an explosion of construction in San Francisco, and the demand for lumber soon gave Rundle and Turner a steady business opportunity. Turner and Rundle spent days exploring the waterfront and the houses of trade. Richard wanted to invest in the lumber trade and talked to those who could give him information on the business. Turner discussed the potential of a shipping business and talked with merchants and captains of vessels that arrived to discharge their cargos. San Francisco was growing fast and had become the absolute center of commerce and industry for the whole Pacific coast.

Turner wanted to buy a ship and become a shareholder in the growth that had to be. He would start small, for he had to learn about the Pacific Ocean before venturing beyond the horizon. Turner was in his happy environment now. Perhaps it was symbolic that his last entry into his diary read:

Sunday, August 21, 1853: Took a sail on the bay.

Turner read an advertisement in the *Daily Alta California* about the "Sign of the Wooden Sailor", a business by Thomas Tennant who made nautical instruments. Turner paid a visit and bought a sextant, a chronometer, and other instruments to navigate a ship.

Figure 10: "Sign of the Wooden Sailor" advertisement.
Source: *Daily Alta California*, September 14, 1853.

Turner began to shop around for a ship and knew exactly what he wanted. In February 1854, he bought the schooner *Toranto*, a small ship of 114 tons and 77.5 feet length of the deck. She was perfect for his first vessel. He had surveyed her and found her sound, although she needed considerable work, including new sails.

Figure 11: The schooner *Toranto*, 1854.
Source: The Hunt Family.

Turner heard that an area called Happy Valley was the best place to work in his newly purchased ship. Happy Valley was located on the shoreline from Mission Street to Rincon Point was an area of "free land" where the early gold seekers of could put up their tents on the sandy beaches at no fee. It was situated where San Francisco's financial district is presently located. It was called Happy Valley because it got lots of sun, provided a natural shelter from winds, and had access to clean, spring water. There were only two ways to get to Happy Valley: one by boat, and the other through the 60-foot-high sandhills that blocked Howard Street and the slopes of Rincon Hill just to the south.[27]

Matthew Turner sailed his new schooner to the shipyard at south shore shipyard. He set up a tent near the shipyard and enjoyed the peaceful surroundings. It was a bustling place for sailors and featured a lagoon with a small shipyard. The residents of Happy Valley lived in tents and wigwams, and the community was known for its peaceful atmosphere. The population was diverse, with people of various nationalities, and it would change from day to day. In the evenings, groups would gather to drink and sing, but there was no excessive drinking. Every day, supply lists were created, and some men would go into the city to make purchases, for which they would be paid a day's wage. Turner would have the men bring him copies of the *Daily Alta California* which he would read after supper.[28]

The *Toronto* was put on the ways where Turner could work on her. She needed new sails that cost 25 cents a yard and 7 cents a yard for sewing. He bought the sail yardage, and two seamen living in the valley cut and sewed the new sails. It took two weeks to replace and re-rig the ship's sails. As soon as Turner was ready to depart on his new ship, he loaded up his belongings and hired the two seamen. One morning after breakfast, they left Happy Valley, picked up Richard Rundle in San Francisco, and set sail for Mendocino.[29]

His plan was to contract with Henry Meiggs, proprietor of the California Lumber Company, to bring lumber from Cape Mendocino to San Francisco using his newly purchased schooner.[30] In April 1854, he arrived in Mendocino with the *Toranto* to pick up a cargo of lumber and return to San Francisco. The storms of late April continued to give all the ships a miserable time as gale-force winds prevailed, which caused a delay in Turner's return to San Francisco.

In July 1854, Turner met Captain Benjamin Franklin Chapman for the first time in Mendocino. Turner learned about the magical islands of the South Seas. Captain Chapman, at 24 years of age, was an authority on the Polynesian waters. He was a self-made man and Turner sensed he was a good businessman. As Captain Chapman prepared his schooner for the voyage back to Tahiti, Turner learned about the importance of lumber and its need in the South Pacific islands.[31]

Turner stayed in Mendocino and talked with his partner, Richard Rundle, about the meetings with Captain Chapman, their talks about the South Seas, and the potential markets Turner was considering exploring. It was at this time that Turner began making his plans for his first trip to San Francisco with a cargo of lumber.[32]

In September 1854, Turner read a newspaper article that his Aunt Mary was in Benicia at the Young Ladies Seminary. This totally surprised and excited him and he planned a visit.

SACRAMENTO DAILY UNION.

THURSDAY MORNING, SEPT. 28.

BENICIA SEMINARY.—Miss Mary Atkins, late of Ohio, has become Principal of the Benicia Female Seminary.

Figure 12: Newspaper article announcing Mary Atkins in Benicia.
Source: *Sacramento Daily Union*, September 28, 1854.

He traveled with his crew from San Francisco to Benicia in his schooner *Toranto*. He made his way past Angel Island, through San Pablo Bay, then along the Carquinez Strait to Benicia. He docked in the same small cove in Benicia where he and Spike Moyes camped one night on their way to Stockton. His men put a small boat over the side to row him ashore. He walked up G Street then over to First Street. He came upon a two-story brick building which was the State Capitol. He walked up the steps and entered the building. He found an attendant which provided directions to get a buggy which would take him to the Young Ladies Seminary. The buggy traveled a short distance on the dirt streets of town and made its way to the Seminary.

The school was a large two-story building of New England Colonial architecture surrounded by a picket fence. Turner used the knocker at front door and was greeted by a woman wondering what his calling was. Matthew identified himself and said he wanted to see Miss Mary Atkins. The matron took him to a book-lined study to wait and get his aunt. When they met there was tearful happiness. They talked through the afternoon, at dinner, and into the evening. Matthew told her of his plans of going to sea, to interesting and exciting places. Later in the evening, Matthew returned to his and hailed his crew for the return to San Francisco.[33]

Figure 13: Mary Atkins Lynch, Matthew Turner's aunt, 1877.
Source: Museum of History Benicia.

Turner made seven trips to Mendocino from June to October 1854 to transport lumber to San Francisco. He always used the California Lumber Company. However, on October 14, 1854, when Turner arrived in San Francisco, he learned that Henry Meiggs had fled to South America after stealing San Francisco city funds and not paying the $1,700 he owed Turner.

Turner decided to change his business and focus on Tahiti. California in 1854 was not a fruit-growing region and was a barren landscape that had little natural produce for its new citizenry. Vitamin C needs could only be met by importing fresh fruit from the South Seas until growers could plant and cultivate their own orchards. With this in mind, Turner would fill this need by trading lumber for fresh fruit.

Turner formed a shipping business partnership with Rundle and they began shipping lumber from the Mendocino coast to Tahiti, and would return with fresh fruit. They used Travers & Clarke and E.P. Adams as agents.

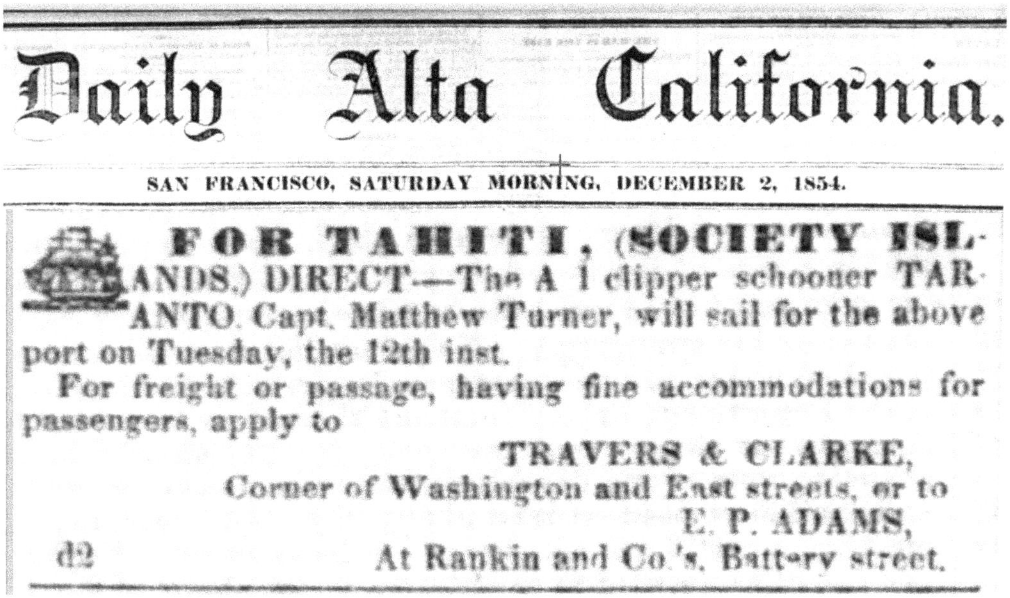

> **Daily Alta California.**
>
> SAN FRANCISCO, SATURDAY MORNING, DECEMBER 2, 1854.
>
> **FOR TAHITI, (SOCIETY ISLANDS,) DIRECT**—The A 1 clipper schooner TARANTO, Capt. Matthew Turner, will sail for the above port on Tuesday, the 12th inst.
>
> For freight or passage, having fine accommodations for passengers, apply to
>
> TRAVERS & CLARKE,
> Corner of Washington and East streets, or to
> E. P. ADAMS,
> At Rankin and Co.'s, Battery street.
>
> d2

Figure 14: Advertisement from the December 2, 1854 *Daily Alta*.
Source: *Daily Alta California* newspaper.

On December 3, 1854, Turner wrote a letter to his father in Ohio describing his interest in the Society Islands.

> *Father dear sir,*
>
> *I cannot recollect when I wrote you last, and it must have been a long time ago. I had nothing to send you, and nothing of interest to write. I am now about to sail on a voyage to the Society Islands, a distance of 4,000 miles, and shall be gone, with ordinary luck, 3 to 4 months. The cargo down will be lumber, and the cargo up oranges and other tropical fruit.*
>
> *You may wonder how, when and where I learned to navigate, or perhaps you think I sail by guess as we used to do on the lakes. The fact is the first time I embarked on salt water I commenced studying the science of navigation, and now with one years practice and experience, I think myself competent to take a vessel to any part of the globe. My vessel is quite old, but otherwise in good order; about an ordinary sailer, not near as fast as the ROBERTS, and I shall put her on the dry dock to clean her bottom and repair her copper before sailing.*
>
> *Henry Meiggs swindled myself and partner, Richard T. Rundle, out of*

$1,700. I have sent home a Daguerreotype to be critically examined, and if not recognized, to be forwarded to Horatio. No letters to me need to arrive before the first of March next.

Lovingly, M. Turner

Needing a larger ship, in November 1855, Matthew sold the *Toronto* and traveled via Panama to Boston where he bought the schooner, *Louis Perry*. The *Louis Perry* was built in Plymouth, Massachusetts in 1853 and was 130 tons capacity, 100 feet length of deck, 9-foot draft, and oak, copper and iron fasteners.

Turner sailed the *Louis Perry* from Boston on the last day of the year and headed for San Francisco by the way of Cape Horn. During the trip, Turner and the crew rescued a group of British sailors who were stranded aboard a steamer called the *Panama*. The British crew was welcomed aboard the *Louis Perry*, and Turner was able to get them to a safe port. This act of high-seas kindness resulted in a personal thank-you gift from Queen Victoria, a gold-mounted spyglass.[34]

In 1856, Turmer decided to take a rare opportunity to test and improve basic seamanship skills for himself and as well for his crew. He would spend the year serving the ports of Buenos Ayres, Argentina, and Valparaiso, Chile, via the Straits of Magellan or around Cape Horn.

The voyage around Cape Horn was 315 miles long but is noted for its stormy passage. The Straits of Magellan was a 115-mile-long passage that was difficult to navigate due to frequent narrows and unpredictable winds and swift currents. This route required intensive vessel handling, navigation skill, patience and time. Turner chose this route and prepared by bringing extra anchors and tie down ropes and lines. Turner made three trips from Buenos Ayres to Valparaiso during the year. He returned to San Francisco on February 15, 1857.[35]

Matthew Turner wanted to continue his trading with Tahiti, but he knew the markets were soft due to the Panic of 1857, so he and his crew planned a voyage to Nikolaevsk, Russia, on the Amur River which flows into the Okhotsk Sea. From the captains that had been up there previously, he knew the type of cargo to carry: tools, knives, guns, clothing, sugar, wheat flour, drugs, and cigars. The trip would be cold and miserable along with choppy seas, and Turner questioned his sanity of such a long trip.[36]

Captain Matthew Turner set sail on the schooner *Louis Perry* from San Francisco to Nicolaevsk in eastern Russia on March 27, 1857. He was carrying an assortment of cargo for trade. Upon arrival on the Asiatic coast, he was detained for three weeks at Castor Bay in the Gulf of Tartary as the Amur River was frozen. During this time, the ship was anchored in 3 fathoms of water, and the crew started fishing with handlines over the rail to make good use of their time. To their surprise, they caught plenty of cod around 2 feet in length.[37] Although Captain Turner had not seen codfish before, some of his crew were familiar with the species, and he realized their market value in San Francisco, which made him interested in fishing for them. With a cargo of furs, the *Louis Perry* sailed for home and arrived in San Francisco on September 17.

The long trip to Nicolaevsk on such a small ship made Turner aware he needed a larger ship for such voyages. Turner sold the *Louis Perry* in 1858 and traveled East again, this time to Newburyport, Massachusetts where he purchased a larger ship, the brigantine *Timandra*.

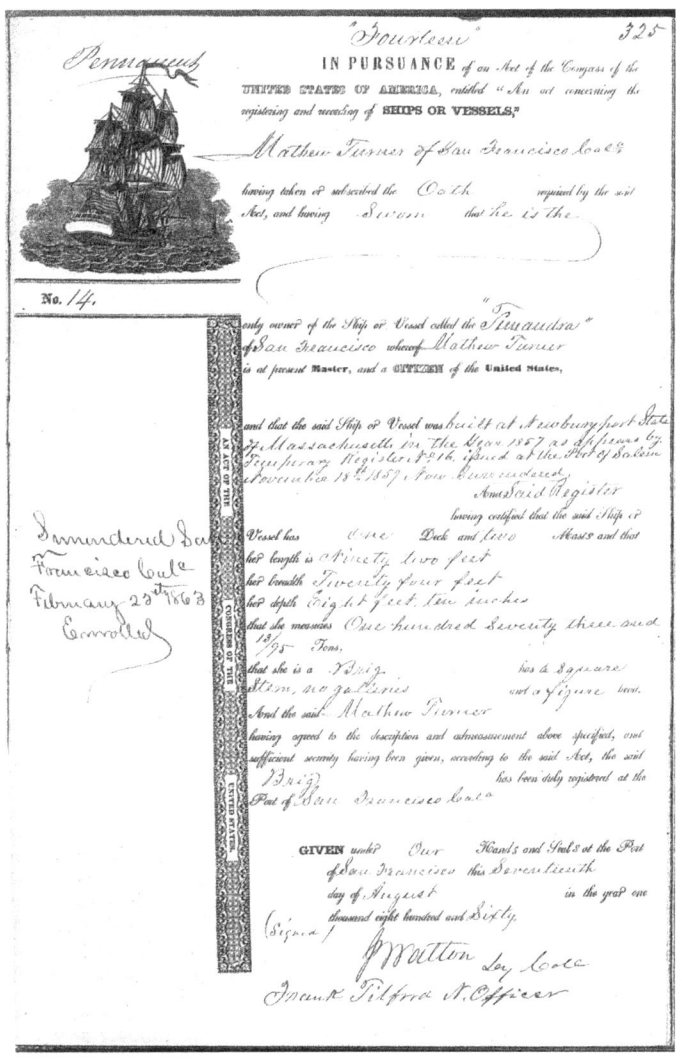

Figure 15: An act of Congress of the United States required that all ships and vessels be registered indicating the name, date of construction, where built, and the owner.

This registration is for the *Timandra* purchased by Matthew Turner on August 17, 1860, and registered as bound for the Port of San Francisco.

Source: The Hunt Family

Figure 16: The brigantine *Winward* shown in this drawing was very similar to the Turner's *Timandra* which he purchased at Newburyport, Massachusetts in 1860.
Source: Illustrated London News, May 1888.

When Turner left Massachusetts to return home on the *Timandra*, he stopped in Boston and brought with him his brother, Horatio, and his two little children, Eva, 7, and Louis, 4. They sailed through the Straits of Magellan and arrived in San Francisco on August 2, 1860.[38]

Turner's lumber market in San Francisco was busy, consuming lumber as fast as it was unloaded from the holds of schooners. Soon, he was transporting lumber and other goods aboard the *Timandra* to markets in the South Pacific Islands.

Richard Rundle ventured into a different aspect of the lumber industry. In 1861, along with William H. Kelley, he built a sawmill at the mouth of Caspar Creek in Mendocino and founded the Caspar Lumber Company. In 1864 the sawmill was purchased by Jacob Jackson and it became the longest-lasting independent lumber mill on the north Mendocino Coast.[39]

In 1861, Horatio married Mary E. Johnson in San Francisco, who had migrated west with her parents from Geneva, New York. They had a daughter, Marion, in 1862 and lived at 335 Beale Street in San Francisco.[40] Horatio would become an active partner in Turner's South Pacific trade business.

San Francisco and Papeete, Tahiti, were Turner's home bases in which the Tahiti Packet Line was operated by Turner and Rundle (later as M. Turner & Co.). Together with a few other sailing firms, their business provided the only regular means of transportation between Papeete and San Francisco for more than thirty years. Papeete-bound cargo consisted of lumber, canned food, and "Yankee notions" (sewing items, scissors, combs, nails, clocks tinware, and other knickknacks). The return cargos were comprised of oranges, coconuts, copra (coconut oil-cake extract), mother-of-pearl, vanilla, and other tropical products. As the cargo was perishable, the competition was tough, as the passage ran between 22 days and 28 days.[41]

The following year he made two trips to Mendocino to see his friend, Richard Rundle. Richard married Ashbeline Mary Smith on April 18, 1863, in Mendocino and later sold his sawmill and moved to San Francisco.[42]

Chapter Five
Matthew Turner's Cod Fishing Journeys

Having experienced the abundance of cod in the Okhotsk Sea region, Captain Turner made another trip to the Amur River in 1863. Turner sailed in his larger brigantine *Timandra*, this time, he brought fishing gear and 25 tons of salt to catch and cure some cod for his return voyage. On the way back, he stopped at the Gulf of Tartary to fish. At first, the cod were plentiful, and 10 tons were caught and salted in kench in just a few days. However, the fish suddenly disappeared, and none could be caught. The brig had to run down the coast to southern Kamchatka, where fish were found in abundance. They had excellent success on the first day, but on the second day, during a dense fog, both anchors were lost. This mishap forced Captain Turner to abandon fishing and return to San Francisco in September where he sold his cod for 15 cents per pound, making his voyage somewhat profitable, with the exception of lost anchors. This was the first time that salt cod had been sold on the west coast from Pacific fishing grounds.[43]

In September 1864, Captain Turner returned to the Okhotsk Sea on another cod-fishing voyage. This time, Turner's crew fished from dories instead of from the deck of the *Timandra*. These dories were designed to be nested on the deck of the vessel and measured approximately 13 feet long at the bottom and 16 feet at the top. Each dory was manned by a single fisherman who would row to his chosen location near the anchored mother vessel and fish with one or two baited hand lines. At the end of the day or when the dory was filled, the fisherman would row back to the mother vessel, where the fish were unloaded, dressed, and salted.

Captain Turner's success inspired others, and in 1865 six fishing vessels sailed from San Francisco to the Okhotsk Sea. An industry had been born. The vessels were small schooners that had been built in New England for the Atlantic fisheries, but had made the journey around Cape Horn to seek codfish in the Pacific Ocean.

On March 27, 1865, Turner set sail to Alaska on the schooner *Porpoise*. He arrived at the Shumagin Islands, located in the Aleutian Islands, on May 1. On the same day, he began fishing and found an abundance of cod close to the shore. He returned to San Francisco on July 7 with a catch of 30 tons of fish, which was less than a full cargo. Although he could have obtained a full cargo, he chose to market the catch in advance of the vessels that had sailed to the fishing grounds on the

Asian side of the Pacific. This catch was the first fare of cod from the Shumagin Islands and has since become famous in the history of Pacific cod fishery.[44]

Newspaper excerpts reported massive amounts of Pacific cod being delivered to San Francisco and the fishery officially had taken off. The account from the *Daily Alta California* in October 1865 depicts a delivery of Alaska cod by Captain Turner, considered by many to be a "pioneer" of the Pacific cod commercial fishing industry.

Daily Alta California

SAN FRANCISCO. FRIDAY MORNING, OCTOBER 27, 1865.

NEW CODFISH.

THE CARGOES OF THE
Brig TIMANDRA, (Captain Turner,)
Schooner H. N. RUGGLES,
Just arrived from the Okhotsh Sea. These fish are well cured, and are far superior to any hitherto brought to this market.
For sale to the trade in lots to suit by
EDMUND MARKS & CO.,
311 Commercial street, near Front.
se2;-nF&Mtf

Figure 17: Newspaper report of Turner's catch of codfish,
Source: *Daily Alta California*, October 1865.

In 1866, the *Timandra* made six codfish trips to the Okhotsk Sea. The total amount for the season was 335 tons of fish. This had the effect of diminishing Eastern importations to a merely nominal figure.[45] In December 1866, the *Timandra* returned to its Tahiti packet line service.

Figure 18: Alaska codfish schooner, circa 1888.
Source: John N. Cobb collection.

Figure 19: Ships at port drying codfish on dock.
Source: Maritime History Archive.

In 1867, reports emerged about the discovery of a "new island" in the Pacific Ocean. The supposed location of the island was along the route of whale ships traveling from Honolulu to Kodiak, Alaska. Captain Turner and his crew aboard the schooner *Caroline Mills* set out on a search and spent three days exploring the area. Despite thorough searching between longitude 149 to 151 west and from latitude 39 to 41 north, no land was found. However, they did come across a patch of discolored water near the reported location of the island and attempted to sound the area but found no bottom down to 120 fathoms (720 feet). On July 1, the *Caroline Mills* returned from the search but set sail again the following day. Although parties involved in the adventure denied that Turner found the island, the fact that the schooner returned without four men suggested that the trip was successful and there was a possibility that they had gone back after finding something on the island.

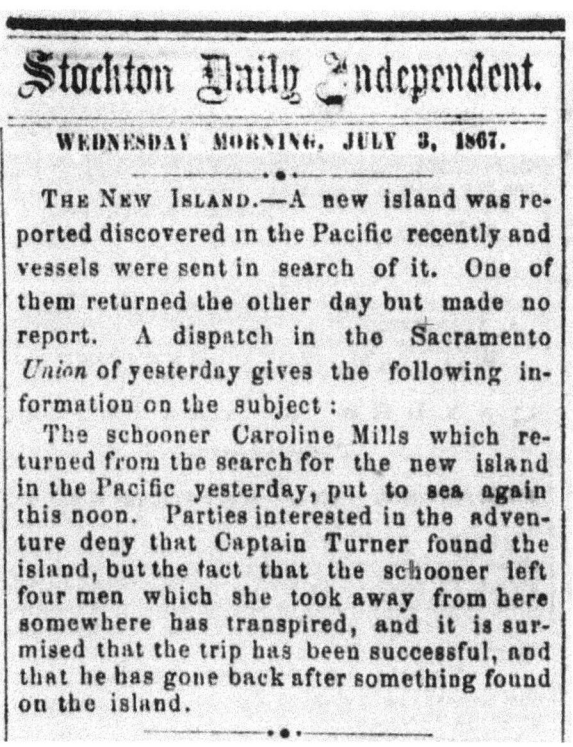

Figure 20: News article on the "New Island" in the Pacific Ocean.
Source: *Stockton Daily Independent*, July 3, 1867.

Matthew Turner's return trip never provided any evidence of a new island. While this topic was debated for several months, there was no new island ever found. Even today, seafloor maps of this area reveal no signs of underwater seamounts or volcanos.

Chapter Six

The Brigantine *Nautilus*[46]

Matthew Turner was about to do what he had done some 20 years earlier: he would design and build his own ship. With his vast sailing experience in the South Seas, around Cape Horn, and across the Pacific Ocean to the Okhotsk Sea, he had a profound understanding of the weather and ocean conditions that a ship must endure.

After the New Year of 1867, Turner and Horatio started preparing for the expansion of their Tahiti packet line business venture. They went to the Wells Fargo Bank in the Parrott Building on the northeast corner of California and Montgomery streets in San Francisco. Matthew made arrangements for the bank to honor Horatio's signature on any drafts he wished to make.

Matthew told Horatio of his plan to find a large warehouse to store their cargoes of lumber, coal, shells, copra, and Sacramento farming country grain. They would then wholesale and retail them to the markets. Matthew would travel to Tahiti to meet with Benjamin Chapman while Horatio would look for a substantial building near Mission Bay, the current shipbuilding area of San Francisco.

Matthew Turner had met Benjamin Chapman on a previous trip to Tahiti. Chapman was a sea captain from New London, Connecticut. He earned his master's certificate at age 18, bought a ship called the *Sea Witch*, and sailed first to the Marquesas Islands, 800 miles northeast of Tahiti in the Pacific. Chapman was now living in Tahiti and they talked about forming a partnership where Turner would furnish the ships to deliver Yankee goods to the islands in return for fruit for Californians.

In Tahiti, Matthew found that Benjamin had bought the brigantine named *Firefly* and was at sea on a trading expedition. Matthew saw the Chapman family was growing: "Charlie" as Benjamin called Adrien, was 9 years old, and their daughter Timandra was 2 years old. The captain did not like the name his wife gave to their son, so he named him Charlie. Charlie would later manage Captain Turner's shipyard in his later years. Matthew said he would return in December to celebrate the holidays with the Chapmans.

Figure 21: Captain Benjamin Chapman (left) and
Adrien Eugene "Charlie" Chapman (right).
Source: The Hunt Family.

Upon returning to San Francisco, Matthew found that Horatio had already set up the "Pacific Produce Agency" with headquarters in a large brick building on Folsom Street, between 16th and 17th streets. He had also moved into a larger house on the corner of Solano and Kentucky streets.

Matthew had planed to return to Tahiti in time to celebrate Christmas with the Benjamin Chapman family. His plans were altered when he received a contract to deliver a cargo of lumber to Callao, Peru, a 4,300-mile run down the coast.

His crew loaded the *Timandra* as quickly as possible, for it was 4,800 miles from Callao back to Tahiti, The day before they departed, Matthew assembled the crew for a talk and said:

> *Gentlemen, we have sailed together for a long time, and you should know of my future plans. We have become aware of the type of ship needed in the Pacific, and she is unlike anything to be had today.*
>
> *She must be shallow, great of beam, and fast, very fast. The barrier between the islands and the mainland will never be conquered until there is such a ship. I have considered this enigma for a long time, and have composed a concept for her.*

> *I want to build the ship I have in mind, and I would like to have you stay with me, and help build and sail her. I would like to ask Captain Chapman to take command of the Timandra during this period, so what do you say?*

For a moment, the crew was startled, but their enthusiasm grew as they discussed the venture. One of the men asked a most important question:

> *Where will you build her, Cap'n. back east?*

> *She will be built right here in California,* Turner answered, *I have been told there is a nest of Cousins brothers up at Humboldt Bay who came from Nove Scotia, and that they are descended from a long line of shipbuilders.*

The crew were unanimous in their support. Captain Turner had been good to them, more than good, for he made them into a family and if he wanted to build a ship, they would help him build her.

They set off to Mendocino to pick up the lumber at the Casper Lumber Company, then set sail for Callao, Peru. As the *Timandra* made her way down the coast, Matthew busied himself making a wooden half-model, from which the shape would be taken for the ship's design. Slowly, he contoured the model from the design in his head, a vision from his 14 years of experience sailing the Pacific Ocean. He held the model in his hands and studied the exquisite curved lines, and knew she would become a ship of infinite character and uniqueness. By the time they reached Callao, the model was complete.

When the lumber delivery was complete, they set sail for Tahiti. On December 23, 1867, they sighted Point Venus at the northern tip of Tahiti and the helmsman set his course around it. The ship entered the Taunoa Pass between the barrier reef and the inner island and focused on Matavai Bay. Soon they saw Pahonu, north of Papeete, where Captain Benjamin Chapman lived. The brigantine *Firefly* was moored at the dock and the helmsman steered the *Timandra* and docked close by.[47]

Upon arrival, the cook went to the lazarette for a keg of rum, and the holiday began. Matthew paid the crew then drank a toast to Christmas with them. Ashore, he was met by Benjamin, Harriet, and young Adrien Chapman.

Matthew began telling Benjamin about his new ship, and he was most excited. His plan was to leave the *Timandra* with Benjamin and return on the *Firefly*. Benjamin suggested putting his friend Captain Wulmot in charge of the *Timandra*. At the Christmas party with Chapmans, Matthew met Captain Wulmot and was impressed. He had a long experience with ships and had fallen in love with the South Pacific islands.

It was a sad day when the crew of the *Timandra* transferred their gear aboard the *Firefly*. Bound for San Francisco, there were a dozen friends and families of Benjamins going along just for the ride. The deck was filled with crates of chickens and pigs. The weather was gentle all the way, and they entertained themselves by dancing and playing with the children.

Before heading to San Francisco, the *Firefly* sailed up the coast to Mendocino to pick up Richard and Ashbeline Rundle. The ship then returned, passing through the Golden Gate strait to reach San Francisco. After the guests disembarked, the Rundles stayed at the Oriental Hotel while Matthew and his crew opted to remain on the ship until their next voyage. Turner resided in the sailmaker's loft and brought his drafting tools with him. He started drawing the lines of the wooden half-model he had carved onto a canvas mat. Whenever he took breaks from his meticulous work, he would read the *Alta California* newspaper. The loft provided a quiet and ideal setting for his work.

When the drawings were complete, Turner made a set of specifications for the ship's sails. He took the drawings to a local sailmaker, and after studying them for a moment the sailmaker said "Cap'n, I ain't ever seen a set of plans like these. Are you sure these are what you want?" Matthew laughed and replied "They are precisely what I want, so get to them and as soon as they are ready you will ship them to Eureka by the brig *Hesperian*. I am going up there with Captain Edwin Brooks Cousins, and will make arrangements with him to bring them up."

Turner boarded the *Hesperian* in the late afternoon, and Captain Cousins invited him to share his quarters. Matthew had become a legend on the San Francisco waterfront, and Captain Cousins wished to have a long talk with him. The brig got under way and before dark she was well offshore and on her way to Eureka. They had supper at the captain's table and talked quite late, and then Matthew climbed into his bunk to have a restful sleep.

It was a two-day journey to Eureka and Captain Cousins timed his arrival with the high tide, and they made their pass over the bar into Humboldt Bay. Ashore, Captain Cousins led the way to his office. There were two framed hulls of medium-sized vessels on the ways and the yard hummed with activity. In the office was a large, broad-shouldered man sitting in a chair with his feet on the desk and a cup of coffee in hand. Turner was introduced by Captain Cousins who said:

Euphronius, this is Captain Turner from San Francisco, and he wants to talk to you about building a new ship.

Euphronius said: *Captain Turner? We have certainly heard of you. Sit down and I will get you a cup of coffee. What type of ship do you intend to build, Captain Turner?*

Turner responded: *A brigantine of about 250 to 260 tons. I want nothing but the best fir to go into her, and no knots in the timbers. I'll show you the plans.*

I have never seen a set of plans like these, said Euphronius.

Turner replied: *I don't imagine you have. My experience in the South Pacific islands brings me to believe this is the ship for work down there. I am willing to invest in my concept to find out. I'd like to bring my crew up here to help work on her. Captain Cousins of the Hesperian arranged for me to employ Captain H. B. Bendixsen to act as superintendent. Would you know of a house we could rent?*

How fancy do you want to live? Houses are quite a distance from the yard, and I have a suggestion. I have a 25' by 35' shed here on the property that can be converted into a place to stay. It won't be fancy, but I can throw up some bunks. I have an old ship's stove I can put in for you to cook on, and keep you warm. All you will need are galley supplies, pots and pans, and your sleeping gear.

I'll buy that. We'll bring our supplies and tools up from San Francisco and while I am gone you can start contracting for the timber, Turner said.

A man, William Carson, has a right good stock of seasoned fir. I have been buying from him, so I will start estimating the materials needed.[48]

Figure 22: Euphronius B. Cousins, owner of the shipyard in Humboldt Bay, circa 1880
Source: San Francisco Maritime National Historical Library.

On the way south to San Francisco, Turner busied himself compiling an inventory of the materials he would need, so he could turn over the list to Horatio. The list included hemp cordage of various sizes for the stays, shrouds, and general rigging and drift bolts, nails, spikes, fore anchors, chain, kedge anchors, capstan, galley equipment, furnishings, compass, binnacle, and housing, hardwood to face the bits, all sizes of hardwood blocks, and the gear for the rudder assembly.

As months passed by, the vessel began to take shape. First came the keel, then the frames, and then the planking. The planking was beautifully fitted, dubbed with an adze, and planed until it felt like a single skin, then caulked and metaled. Internally, strong wood knees (curved wood braces) were used to support the deck beams. The bottom was painted black to the waterline, and white above which glistened like snow in the sunlight.

The spars and bowsprit had been shaped, and the material for the masts, made to precise specifications in San Francisco, were oiled and fitted to the masts. When stepped, the masts would rise 119 feet into the air. The last item to go aboard was a black-plated name board which had been carved with her name and the letters covered and burnished in gold leaf.

On November 18, 1868, at 11 a.m., a crowd assembled for the launching, and Turner raised a bottle of champagne and struck it across the bow. "I name thee *Nautilus*." Turner was proud. The ship was 115 feet in length, 21 feet across in beam, and drew 10 feet 6 inches.

> *Gentlemen. I have a feeling we have a ship here. Tomorrow morning at 8 o'clock we will take her out and see what she will do.*

All were up at dawn, and preparations were made to take the *Nautilus* out for the first time. Each crew member double-checked the position of their equipment, as there were multiple working parts that each crew member was responsible for. Once they were satisfied with everything, they headed to the galley to have breakfast.[49]

Captain Cousins arrived at 7:30 am and the tow tug was ready at 8:00. The crew took the tow line aboard and fastened it to the ship's docking post, and were towed into Humboldt Bay.

Figure 23: Humboldt Bay had a sandbar across the entrance making it accessable only at low tides. Today the entrance has been dredged.
Source: Robert Campbell, U.S. Army Corps of Engineers.

As the tug moved them out into open water, the Bermudian main sail and the ringtail top sail were raised. With the dropping of the tow line, up went the sails, and the foresails were sheeted fast. Matthew was at the helm and he watched the heads of the sails and called his commands to set the rope lines.

The *Nautilus* responded faster than any other ship Matthew had sailed. The design allowed her to pivot closer to the bow than he had dreamed she would. At the south end of the bay, he gave the command to come about and swung the wheel. The action was instant as the crew worked fast to adjust the sails.

Captain Cousins was given the helm. Despite the fairly strong winds, she stood straight up, and he realized why Captain Turner had given her the wide beam and designed the masts the way he had. The rest of the day was spent preparing for the run south to San Francisco. Matthew was going to take the *Nautilus* down to Tahiti and back, and her performance would determine how far they would go with this design concept.

On December 2, the *Nautilus* was towed into the bay at 5:30 a.m. At 6:00 a.m., the *Nautilus* passed over the bar into the Pacific Ocean. Matthew set the course and, one by one, the crew took turns at the helm. The weather was good and they could not believe the speed she skimmed over the water.

At 8 o'clock in the morning of December 4, the *Nautilus* entered the San Francisco Bay. She moved swiftly down the bay and passed the Jackson Street wharf where they saw the *Firefly* docked. Matthew made a port tack out into the bay and came about and ran up toward Angel Island. He then and made another run toward the waterfront. The crew began lowering the sails to make a gentle approach to Mission Bay wharf. By the time she was moored, the wharf was crowded with spectators admiring the snow-white hull and towering canvas sails.

Matthew's plan for the maiden voyage of the *Nautilus* was a round trip to Tahiti. He studied and plotted the course with care, intending to make as fast a round trip as possible. That was the purpose of the *Nautilus* design and he would find out if she was the ship she was designed to be.[50]

The cargo for the maiden voyage was loaded into the ships hold. The date for launch was set for December 12. At 10 o'clock in the morning, the fore sails went up and the *Nautilus* cast off, taking advantage of the outgoing tide and the light north-westerly winds. When she made her way into the wind, the other sails were raised and she began to move swiftly. The *Nautilus* went out through the Golden Gate and past Fort Point, as the crew set about setting and adjusting all sails as she entered the Pacific Ocean.

Matthew set her course to take them into the California current which would carry them to 900 miles north of the equator. There they would come into the influence of the east-west North Equatorial current which would carry them to the Equatorial counter current flowing eastward. Past the equator, they would come into the influence of the westerly flowing South Equatorial current that would take them down to Tahiti.

Matthew and the crew were pleased with the *Nautilus's* performance, even in rough weather. Her balance was beautiful, and most of the time the ship went where they wanted her to go, instead of where the winds and currents wished to take her.

On December 29, 1868, they entered the main channel into Papeete Bay at 10 o'clock in the morning and began lowering the sails for docking. They had arrived in Tahiti. The crew gathered in the captain's cabin and asked:

> *How'd we do, Cap'n?*

> *Gentleman, it looks like we have set a bit of a record. We made the run from San Francisco to Papeete Bay in exactly 17 days, to the hour. Our average was 235.5 miles a day, with a top of 298 miles. You have something to be proud of. You have all earned a month's pay as a bonus, so go have a time for yourselves. You have made history.*[51]

The *Nautilus* was decorated with garlands of flowers each day, and New Years Eve was unlike anything Matthew had ever known. It was open house at the Chapman's, and many distinguished members of Tahitian families paid their respects. They brought him gifts of appreciation for becoming part of their life and the service he rendered to their people.

The *Firefly* arrived early in the morning on January 2, 1869, and moored abaft the *Nautilus*. When Benjamin asked what her transit time was on the down-passage, he whistled and accepted a cup of grog to toast the beauty all over again.

Matthew and Benjamin discussed the need for inner-island schooners, and concluded that Benjamin would take command of the *Nautilus* after they arrived in San Francisco. Matthew would return to Eureka and begin building schooners needed for the inner-island trade.

Matthew had set a sailing date of January 12 for the return trip to San Francisco. He was going to drive the *Nautilus* to maximum capacity without straining and endangering her. He wanted to establish a routine drive that would be her potential, for she was designed and built to take this routine as common procedure.

On the morning of January 12, the quay at Papeete was lined with mariners and townspeople who had come to give their good wishes and to present a pennant of the Red Cockerel to the *Nautilus* for her 17-day voyage down to Tahiti. Matthew thanked them, and a crew member proceeded to hoist the sixty-foot-long flag to the top of the mainmast.[52]

The *Nautilus* set sail and worked her way into the wind stream as the sails were quickly set. She made her way through the pass, flying her pennant which danced in the wind high above the ship. Then she began to sail northward bound for San Francisco.

Figure 24: The brigantine *Nautilus*, circa 1870.
Source: San Francisco Maritime National Historical Library.

On the morning of January 31, 1869, the *Nautilus* sailed into the San Francisco Bay with all sails set, including her stun'sails and pennant. She was carried by the tide and winds as she glided into the Bay. She was a beautiful thing outlined boldly against the cloudless blue sky and many a crew and early risers were witnessing something extraordinary.

The return trip was 19 days and word passed that the *Nautilus* had returned from Tahiti with a cargo of fresh fruit and vegetables, and bidding for the cargo went sky high. The wharf was so jammed with the curious that it was difficult to unload her cargo.

The maiden voyage of *Nautilus* did not go unnoticed. The *Alta California* published an article about the facts of the trip.

Journey of the Brigantine *Nautilus*, Maiden Voyage
San Francisco-Tahiti; Tahiti-San Francisco
Departure S.F: December 12, 1868, 10 a.m.
Enter Papeete: December 29, 1868, 10 a.m.
(17 days down)
Depart Papeete: January 12, 1869, 6 a.m.
S. F.: January 31, 1869, 6 a.m.
(19 days up)
Total sailing days, round trip: 36
Average miles per day down: 233
High day's run down: 298.0
Average miles per day up: 210.5
Average miles for trip: 222.4

Matthew hired a schooner to go north to Mendocino Bay to fetch Richard and Ashbeline Rundle to San Francisco for a celebration. Sitting in the Captain's room on the return trip, Matthew, Horatio, and Benjamin discussed the plans for the continued success of their business. Matthew was to continue building ships, so the *Nautilus* needed to be allowed to prove the value of her concept. It was concluded that the *Nautilus* would not carry lumber, but would ply back and forth between San Francisco and Tahiti to establish her capability as the fastest packet operating the two ports. She would carry passengers and general cargo, and when they were satisfied, they would apply for French and American mail contracts. By that time, Benjamin could put a competent Master aboard, and devote himself to the new ships Matthew would be delivering to Tahiti for inner-island trade.

When the schooner returned to San Francisco with the Rundles, they moored next to the *Nautilus* and Richard saw her for the first time. He stood on the wharf and studied her, feeling some of the excitement that Matthew must have felt when he said that he was going to bring into being his first child, and she was going to be beautiful.

The Rundles were escorted on deck. Richard stood on deck and looked up to see the top of her slender foremast. They were then shown to *Nautilus'* Captain's cabin where Matthew and Benjamin greeted them. "Richard, Ashbeline, come in,"

Matthew said. The cabin was kept warm by a coal fire in the hearth of the fireplace. Benjamin poured a rum drink for both of them, and they raised their glasses and said "To Matthew, and the *Nautilus*."[53]

They talked all afternoon, enjoying sandwiches, coffee, and warm spice. Matthew explained his plan of returning to Mendocino to build a series of 30 to 100-ton schooners for the inner-island trade, and Benjamin would take command of the *Nautilus*. Richard would remain in San Francisco running the business with Horatio and Benjamin would be in Tahiti expanding their packet line industry.

A new era in shipbuilding began. Matthew Turner studied the characteristics of the Pacific Ocean and he found that they differed significantly from the Atlantic Ocean in terms of weather conditions and prevailing winds. To reflect these differences, he designed the hull and sails of the *Nautilus* accordingly. Turner introduced a unique hull design that combined a very long and sharp bow with a full run. The full run refers to the shape of the after part of the ship's underbody, which relates to the resistance it generates as it moves through the water. The design also incorporated little or moderate deadrise, which is the angle of the rise of a ship's bilge from the horizontal. The longer bow allowed it to cut through the sea, preventing the forward part of the ship from losing its steerage and creating more maneuverability.

Turner's design improved both the speed and stiffness of the ship. Turner's ships had a characteristic sharp, forward-raking stem with little sheer above the waterline. He placed the heavy windlass machinery and the catheads, which are usually found in the bow, farther aft than was common. This helped take the weight off the long, narrow bow and distribute it to where the hull was broader.[54]

One of his most notable enhancements was the use of one-piece masts made from the tall trees found on the Pacific Coast. Additionally, he introduced the triangular "Bermuda" sail as the after-most fore and aft sails on Pacific ships. This was a significant change from the previously used sail types, which were used on ships carrying fore and aft rigs, such as brigantines and barkentines, in addition to schooners. The triangular Bermuda sail allowed Turner to remove the long gaff, reducing damage and strain on the ship.[55]

In March 1879, Turner sold the *Nautilus* to Captain Stephen Higgins, the ship's former captain, for $8,000.[56]

In August 1895, the *Nautilus* was heading towards Hereheretue Island, an atoll located 230 miles southeast of Tahiti in the South Pacific. The rough seas made it extremely difficult to land. As the *Nautilus* approached the island, the winds suddenly changed direction from west to east, causing the ship to wreck during the landing. After 27 years of serving the Tahiti Packet Line, the *Nautilus* finally ended its service.[57]

CHAPTER SEVEN
Matthew Turner's Shipyard in San Francisco

Matthew Turner started with the building of inner-island schooners for Tahiti. In 1870, he began building the *Island Belle*, a schooner of 41 tons capacity, in San Francisco. The ship was completed in December and immediately began its packet line service to Tahiti in January 1871. Five more packet line schooners were built from 1872 to 1874 in Eureka.[58]

In 1875, Matthew Turner officially opened his shipyard at the end of Sixth Street,[59] in the area of Mission Bay, San Francisco. Turner took up residence at The Windsor Hotel, 905 Market Street.

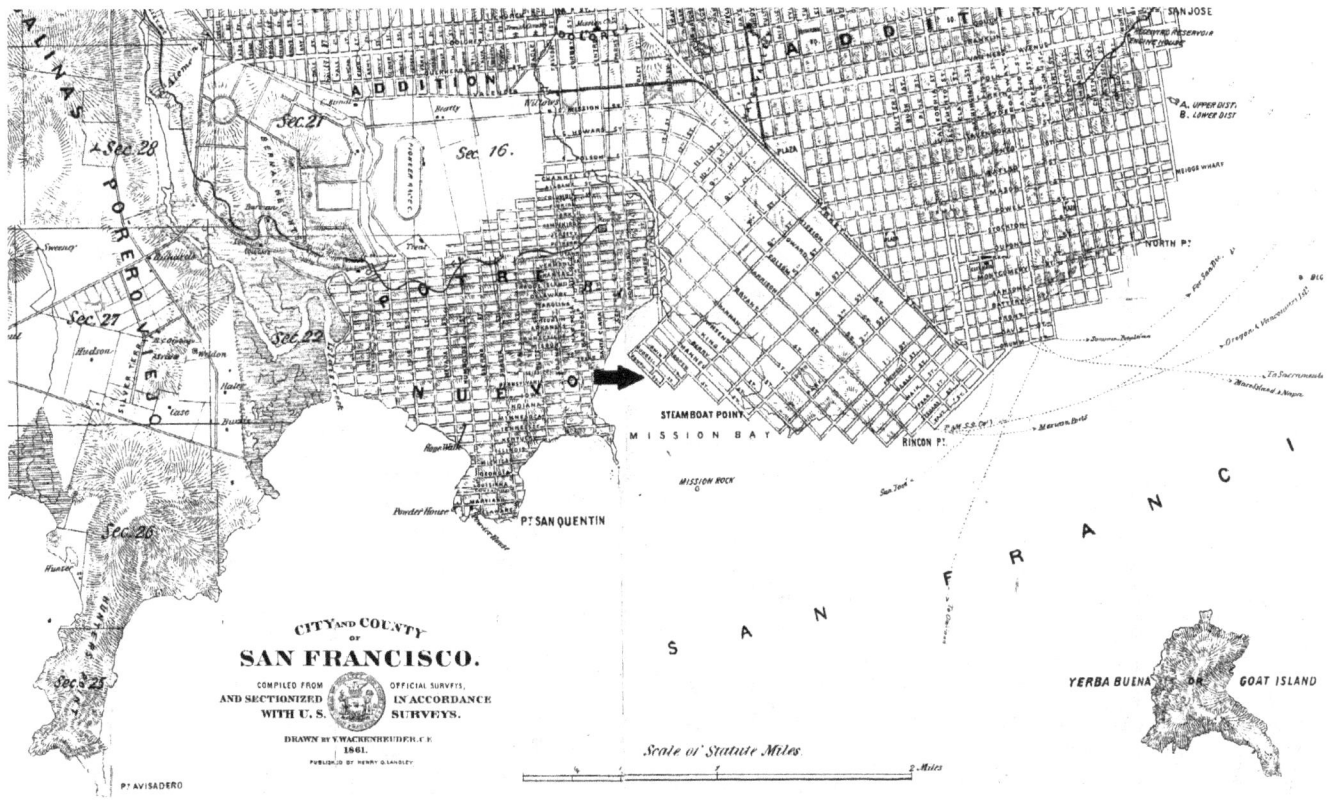

Figure 25: 1861 map of the site of Matthew Turner's shipyard at the end of Sixth Street, Mission Bay area in San Francisco (arrow). Source: Drawn by V. Wackenreuder, 1861.

There were a mix of small and large shipyards in the Mission Bay area. The steamer vessels were constructed along a stretch of bay coastline called "Steamboat Point." The shipbuilders at Steamboat Point at time were Henry B. Tichenor (at the foot of Second Street), Patrick Henry Tiernan (at the foot of Third Street), John G. North (at the foot of Third and Fourth streets). William I. Stone, another well-known shipbuilder, had a shipyard across Mission Bay at Shasta and Illinois Streets. Matthew Turner's shipyard was located at the foot of Sixth Street in 1870.

Figure 26: Henry B. Tichenor's Shipyard pictured above, located at Second Street (near Matthew Turner's shipyard at Sixth Street), 1865. In the distance is Goat Island (now called Yerba Buena Island).
Source: San Francisco Maritime National Historical Library.

In 1871, Turner traveled to Tahiti on the schooner *Island Belle*. His crew list included his half-brother George E. Turner, age 27, Horatio's son Louis H. Turner, age 14, and a friend Joseph Isaacs, age 14. George E. passed away in San Francisco the following year at age 28.

> **Crew List from Customs Records Group 36, January 24, 1871.**
>
> *Master: Matthew Turner, Ohio. age 45*
> *Mate: Geo. E. Turner, Ohio. age 27, wage $40*
> *Seaman: Jos. W. Isaacs, New Jersey. age 14. wage $15*
> *Seaman: L. H. Turner, Illinois. age 14, wage $15.*

Figure 27: Crew List from the *Island Belle* voyage to Tahiti on January 24, 1871.
Source: US Archives, Customs Record Group 36.

The first ship that Turner built for a customer was the half-brigantine *Siberia*, which was commissioned by Lindholm & Co. of Vladivostok, Russia. It was launched in March 1875 at B. F. Webster shipyard in Mission Bay, San Francisco. A trial trip was made with thirty passengers from the Jackson Street wharf in San Francisco to Oakland and back. The *Siberia* was the first of four vessels built in San Francisco to be equipped with steam engines. Turner contracted the Fulton Iron Works to install the steam engines.

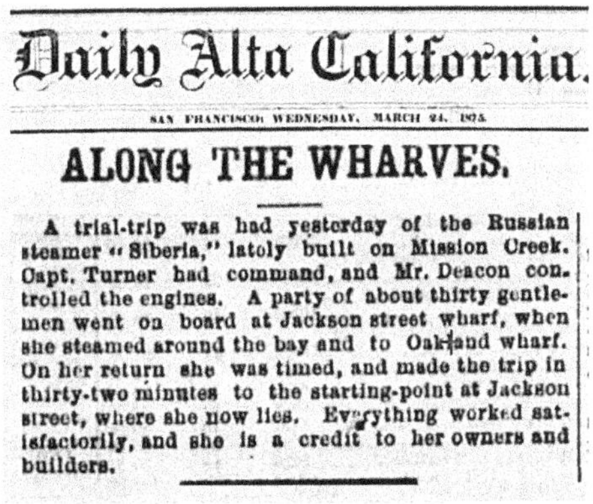

Daily Alta California.

SAN FRANCISCO, WEDNESDAY, MARCH 24, 1875.

ALONG THE WHARVES.

A trial-trip was had yesterday of the Russian steamer "Siberia," lately built on Mission Creek. Capt. Turner had command, and Mr. Deacon controlled the engines. A party of about thirty gentlemen went on board at Jackson street wharf, when she steamed around the bay and to Oakland wharf. On her return she was timed, and made the trip in thirty-two minutes to the starting-point at Jackson street, where she now lies. Everything worked satisfactorily, and she is a credit to her owners and builders.

Figure 28: Newspaper article of the steamer *Siberia* trial trip.
Source: *Daily Alta California* March 25, 1875.

On May 4, 1875, Turner launched his first ship from his Mission Bay shipyard, a 60-ton schooner named *Alata* for his Hawaii trade route. By this time, Turner's reputation was well established, and he began an impressive period of production, launching eight vessels per year for the following eight years. Turner set up his office at 122 California Street in San Francisco and began accepting orders for vessels. Orders were placed through a contract, which included a detailed list of specifications and pricing. After the vessel was launched and a trial sailing was completed, it was handed over to the buyer.

Below is an example of a contract between Matthew Turner and the Wilkens Company of San Francisco for the schooner *Henry*.[60]

Specifications Schooner Henry, May 15, 1891
Specification of Material and manner of building a Schooner called Henry after the model of the schooner Mabel Scott (50 tons US-Register)
Dimensions 83 ft long, 22 ft beam, 7 ft 3" depth of hold
Keel 12" x 24" including shoe
Stern side 12" and mould 15"
Stern Post 16" x 16" sided to 7" at top of keel

Dead Wood sided 12" and moulded of sufficient depth to receive the heels of the cants

Frames Spaced 27" from center to center, mould 10" at keel 6" at deck, timbers sided 8" fastened to keel with one 4" bolt

Keelson 12" x 24" in one piece fastened with two 7/8" bolts to each frame, driven from top of keelson to bottom of keel

Ceiling 3" from keelson to lower turn of bilge, fastened with galvanized, spikes. From thence to deck 4" thick fastened with one 9" spike and one 4 bolt to each plank and frame Clamps 6" x 12" worked onto ceiling and fastened with composition spikes and Locust treenails to 7 ft draft, from thence to deck fastened with galvanized. spikes and Locust treenails. Deck beams 7" x 10" fastened to clamps and ceiling with 7/8" bolts to each end of every beam.

Partner and Hatch Beams shall have hanging knees.

Bulwarks 1 1/4" x 4" T & G Pine fastened with galvanized. nails

Rail 4" x 9" fastened with one 8" galvanized. spike to each stanchion

Cabin Extending from side to side at height of rail and 15 ft fore and aft. Sliding doors to divide the cabin.

Forward part to be fitted with berth on one side and trade room with shelves on the other.

After part shall have two berths and W.C. on the Port side and one berth and pantry on the other side two port lights on each side.

Forecastle & Galley in a house on deck

Rudder Stock of Oak 9" diameter

Steerer Reeds Patent

Windlass Patent pump break 16"purchase

Anchors One of 550, one of 450 and one of 150 lbs.

Chains 45 fathoms 7/8" chain and 45 fathoms 3/4" chain and 60 fathoms of 4" rope for ketch warp

Sails Mainsail, Foresail and Jib of No. 2, Flying jib of 4 outer jub of No. 6 and staysail of No.8 cotton duck

Rigging Standing rigging wire rope 4 shrouds to the fore and 3 shrouds to the mainmast of 2 3/4" rope

Caulking Vessel shall be well caulked and made tight

Spars of Oregon Pine good material and properly made

Metal 16, 18 and 20 oz. up to 7 1/2 feet draft

Boat one 16 foot boat with oars

Paint two coats of white lead paint outside and in the cabin

Galley stove and cooking utensils, dishes for cabin, spirit compass, Anchor and Sidelights,
Foghorn, lead and line, one flag, water casks of 500 gallons capacity.

This agreement entered into on the 15th day of May 1891, by and between Matthew Turner of the first part and Wilkens & Co. of the second part, both of the City of San Francisco. Witnesseth: that the party of the first part agrees to build for the party of the second part, a schooner in a good and workmanlike manner, of good material and in accordance with the proceeding specifications and deliver her in the harbor of San Francisco on or before the 30th day of July next for the sum of . . . ., in consideration of which the party of the second part agrees to pay unto the party of the first part the sum of . . . . on signing this agreement . . . . when the vessel is in frame and true and faithful delivery of the vessel.
In witness whereof we have hereunto set our hands the day and year above written
Signed
Matthew Turner
Wilkens Co.

The shipbuilding details were delivered to the Turner shipyard for preparation of the construction. As it later turned out, however, the *Henry* ended up costing $7,920 US gold without copper skin instead of the mentioned $5,200 metal included.

Once the contract was fulfilled and the ship was delivered, Turner was required to complete a "Master Carpenter's Certificate" per the General Customs Regulations. This document established a ship's origin and ownership.

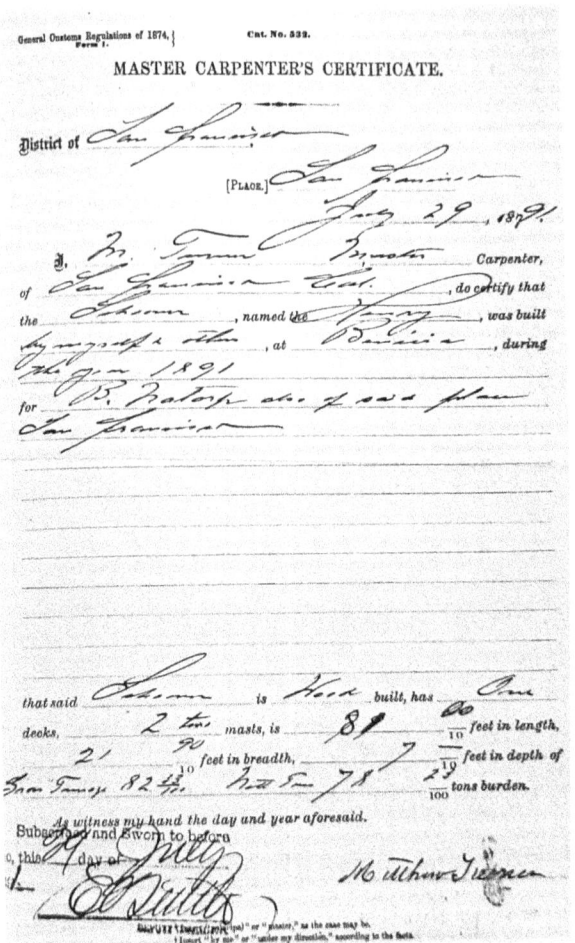

Figure 29: Master Carpenter's Certificate for the schooner *Henry*.
Source: San Francisco Maritime National Historical Library.

The South Pacific Ocean gained the attention of Europe in the latter half of the 18th century, and contact with the islands of French Polynesia occurred gradually. The Society Island groups, primarily Tahiti, became a French protectorate in 1842 and a colony in 1880. The islands had a demand for lumber, in which fruit and copra could be offered in return. There was a need for fast travel to transport fresh fruit back to San Francisco.

With the brigantine *Nautilus*, Matthew Turner started a business offering travel from San Francisco to Tahiti. On December 9, 1868, the *Daily Alta California* carried an advertisement for travel to Tahiti and the Society Islands on the new clipper brig, *Nautilus*, with Matthew Turner, Master.

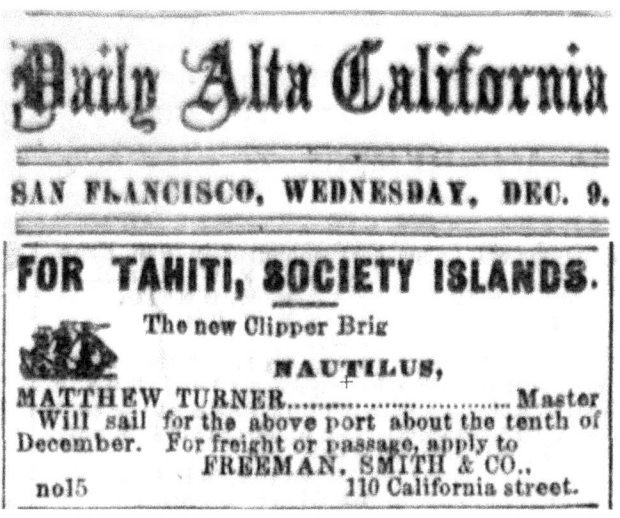

Figure 30: Advertisement in the newspaper for the new Clipper Brig *Nautilus*. Source: *Daily Alta California*, December 9, 1868

Many of Turner's first vessels were destined for the Society Islands. Between 1870 and 1883, nineteen schooners were built for the Tahiti trade at Turner's San Francisco Mission Bay and Eureka shipyards.

Japan also took an interest in Matthew Turner's ships. In 1874, the Japanese Government requested through their Consulate in San Francisco to have a copy of the plans, specifications, and models of Turner's vessels. It was believed that the adaptation of this style of vessel would be the means of saving hundreds of lives annually that are now endangered by the insufficiency of the bulky and unwieldy Japanese vessels in stormy seas. The request was honored by sending the documents of three schooner brigantines, two schooners, and one sloop model. The vessels were of different sizes, the tonnage varying from 20 to 200 tons. Among the drawings and specifications, two were those of the brigantine *Nautilus* and the schooner *Atalanta*.[61]

The Karluk River is situated on the southwestern end of Kodiak Island, Alaska, and is known for its vast Sockeye Salmon runs. The region has been home to the

Alutiiq people for generations, who traditionally lived a coastal lifestyle, relying mainly on salmon supplemented with abundant land resources. In 1876, the Karluk Packing Company of Alaska started purchasing schooners to fish for salmon at the Karluk River and ship them to Pacific Coast ports, which included fifteen Matthew Turner vessels. The company was funded by the Alaska Commercial Company, a grocery and retail company that operated stores in rural Alaska. In 1882, the first cannery opened on Kodiak Island, and the Karluk Packing Company began shipping canned salmon to Pacific ports.

The German Government entered the South Pacific trading business in 1884. However the late point of entry forced Germany to take what trading areas were left, the northeastern New Guinea and the Bismarck Archipelago. These resource-poor and scattered territories were not ideal for maintaining a substantial business, yet, Germany ordered sixteen schooners from Matthew Turner.

From 1875 to 1883, Matthew Turner resided at 711 Tennessee Street, San Francisco, in the Richard Rundle home, located approximately half a mile from the shipyard at the end of Sixth Street across Mission Bay. His office was located at 122 California Street.

Figure 31: Matthew Turner's residence at 711 Tennessee Street in San Francisco, circa 1880. Matthew is on the porch (near the left side). Source: The Hunt Family.

In 1876, Richard Rundle passed away leaving his wife Ashbeline to fend for her three children, George (12), Charlotte (10), and Eva (6).

In 1878, at the age of 53, Matthew's family situation changed when he married Ashbeline Rundle in a civil ceremony in San Francisco. Turner had promised Rundle he would take care of his family. Matthew was a devoted husband, father, and grandfather, and he and Ashbeline were married for 28 years.

Figure 32: Matthew Turner (age 53) and Ashbeline Mary Rundle (age 35), circa 1878.
Source: Vaughan Photographic Gallery, San Francisco (Matthew) and The Hunt Family (Ashbeline).

Figure 33: Charlotte Jane Rundle (left), George Granger Rundle (center), and Eva Turner Rundle (right), circa 1878.
Source: Vaughan Photography, 18 Third Street, San Francisco, courtesy of the Museum of History Benicia.

Captain Turner, Commodore John Eckley, and Commander A. E. Chapman were all yacht racing enthusiasts. In the early 1870s, they sailed the San Francisco Bay and according to an 1891 *San Francisco Chronicle* article reports that Turner was considered the best sailor on the bay in his open sloop, the *Molly Woggin*. "He always sails in his shirtsleeves, no matter what the weather," the *Chronicle* stated, adding Turner "isn't afraid of anything in the way of an aerial disturbance."

Turner loved to sail the new schooners that he had built. The *Daily Alta California* newspaper released the following article about the new schooner *Rosario* in May 1878.

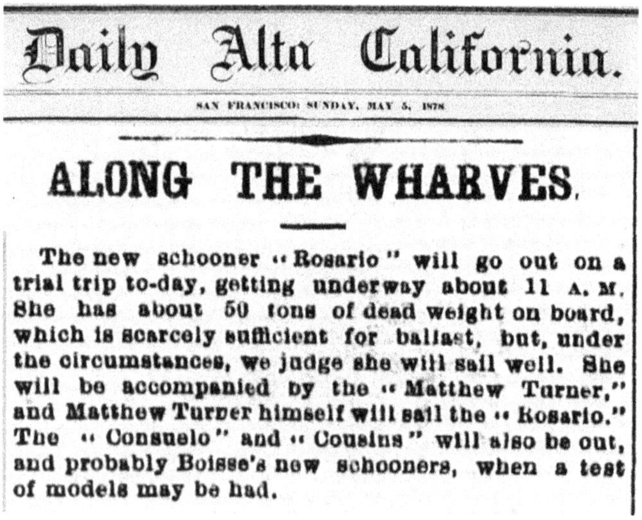

Daily Alta California.

SAN FRANCISCO: SUNDAY, MAY 5, 1878

ALONG THE WHARVES.

The new schooner "Rosario" will go out on a trial trip to-day, getting underway about 11 A. M. She has about 50 tons of dead weight on board, which is scarcely sufficient for ballast, but, under the circumstances, we judge she will sail well. She will be accompanied by the "Matthew Turner," and Matthew Turner himself will sail the "Rosario." The "Consuelo" and "Cousins" will also be out, and probably Boisse's new schooners, when a test of models may be had.

Figure 34: Announcement of Turner's new schooner *Rosario*.
Source: *Daily Alta California,* May 5, 1878.

Sometimes the ships don't end up as they were intended. Twenty years later, the *Rosario*, originally built for the Tahiti and Hawaii trade routes, ended up as a whaling vessel. On July 2, 1898, it was crushed in the ice off Point Barrow on the northern tip of Alaska. Captain E. Coffin described the final moments:

> *We were forced bodily on the shore Ice, our rudder carried away, the masts ground to splinters and the Rosario was turned on her side to an angle of 38 degrees with the ice. The crush came so quickly we were obliged to leave the ship at once if we wished to save ourselves. She kept careening from one side to the other and finally settled. on her stern with the bow up in the air. the ice. eight to ten feet in thickness, forcing her up. We had just five minutes to get out and not even the ship's chronometer was saved. For thirty days we lived in tents alongside the ship and could do nothing to save her from being ground up in the ice.*[62]

Figure 35: The *Rosario* in ice, July 1, 1898.
Source: San Francisco Maritime National Historical Library, Walter A. Scott.

Daily Alta California.

SAN FRANCISCO: MONDAY, MAY 6, 1878.

A TEST OF SPEED.

The "Matthew Turner" Outsails All Her Rivals.

Yesterday being a fine day, with a good breeze, the schooner *Matthew Turner*, with her owner on board, and a party of invited guests, "Along the Wharves" among them, got under way, from her anchorage in Mission Bay, and proceeded down the harbor. She was followed soon after by Turner's latest, the schooner *Rosario*, sailed by Captian Turner himself, and had over a hundred people on board. Both vessels presented a fine appearance, as they passed along the front, and on reaching North Point Dock, they picked up the little *Consuelo*, and one and all went after Boisse's new schooner, which, at the time, was about a mile ahead of the *Turner*, and, with a good breeze, was evidently doing her level best. Nothing daunted, however, the *Matthew Turner* trimmed her sheets well aft, Gutte "piped all hands" to grog, and the effects were soon visible. On reaching Black Point, the *Turner* was up with her rival, and to windward withal, and continuing down. When the *Turner* was a half-mile outside the Fort, Boisse's schooner was barely abreast of the Presidio, with the *Rosario* and *Consuelo* a mile below and to windward of her. We think this is a fair test of what Turner's models are, and all must agree that they can't be beat.

Figure 36: Announcement about a race in the San Francisco Bay.
Source: *Daily Alta California,* May 6, 1878.

Turner continued to operate his Tahiti Packet Line business with Captain Benjamin Chapman. Chapman managed the business in Papeete, Tahiti, at the office located on Main Street which served as the shipping trade business and schooner operations center. The business arranged shipping trades from the South Pacific to San Francisco and the North American ports from 1870 to 1900.

Figure 37: The Turner and Chapman business (center) in Papeete, Tahiti, circa 1880.
Source: The Hunt Family

In 1880, John Diedrich Spreckels organized J. D. Spreckels and Brothers, a company to establish a trade between the mainland United States and the Hawaiian Islands. The company began with one sailing vessel, the *Rosario*, and later controlled two large fleets of sail and steam vessels. The shipping and passenger line of this enterprise was the Oceanic Steamship Company founded in 1881, and was also engaged extensively in sugar refining, and became agents for leading sugarcane plantations in Hawaii. In 1926, the Oceanic Steamship Company sold out to Matson Line and became a subsidiary company. Turner built eight ships for John Spreckels, the *Rosario*, the *Claus Spreckels*, the *John D. Spreckels*, the *Consuelo*, *W. H. Dimond*, the *Anna*, the *William G. Irwin*, and the *Lurline*. The *Lurline* was Turner's most famous yacht, built in 1883 for John D. Spreckels. She was sold to H. H. Sinclair of Los Angeles in 1904 and was lengthened and deepened for racing.

Figure 38: The half-brigantine, *John D. Spreckels*, 266 tons capacity built in 1880 at the Turner shipyard in San Francisco. Source: Felix Reisenberg, Jr., 1940.

The year 1879 became the first year Matthew Turner was listed in the San Francisco Directory as a shipbuilder. It took 11 years, from his first packet *Nautilus* in 1868, until the Spreckels order of *Claus Spreckels* in 1879 to achieve this recognition.

The scow schooner *Theresa* was built in 1882 and purchased by Miss Celia P. Lewis. She was described as a sweet-faced little woman who was familiar with every "water-fronter" along the docks. She ran a lively delivery business with stops in San Francisco, Vallejo, Benicia, and Sacramento. She hired her own crew, attended to all shipping, solicited all orders, and settled all bills. She was a common sight along the docks with her shipping receipt book in hand, tallying off a cargo of merchandise while big burly truck drivers awkwardly stood by with undistinguished curiosity and astonishment.[63]

In January 1883, it was announced that Turner would be moving his shipyard to Benicia, partnering with Commodore Isadore Gutte, Captain Gustave Niebaum, and Commodore John Eckley. Turner would continue to live in San Francisco and operate his shipyard and his Tahiti packet line.

PLACER HERALD.

OFFICIAL PAPER OF PLACER COUNTY,
AUBURN, JANUARY 13, 1883.

Capt. Matthew Turner, the ship-builder, I. Gutte, G. Niebaum and John Eckley have formed a partnership and have purchased 40 acres of land opposite Port Costa and a little below Benecia. It is their intention to start a ship-building yard on the ground, and from all appearances it will be a splendid place, as there is fine water there and the land is well adapted for the purpose, while the cost for transportation of material will be trifling. It is the intention of the parties mentioned to launch at once into the venture, and build vessels that will "astonish the natives."

Figure 39: Newspaper announcement on January 13, 1883 of Matthew Turmer moving his San Francisco shipyard to Benicia.
Source: *Placer Herald*, January 13, 1883.

Figure 40: Commodore Isador Gutte
Source: San Francisco Maritime National Historical Library.

Chapter Eight
Matthew Turner Shipyard Moves to Benicia

In 1883, the Union Works needed more space for building mining machinery and the construction of steel vessels, so Matthew Turner was forced to move out of his San Francisco shipyard.[64] He selected an ideal site in Benicia to relocate his shipyard which was along the deepwater channel Carquinez Strait. Except for the distance from his office at 122 California Street in San Francisco, the site at Benicia was perfect for launching ships because the bedrock was extended to the shoreline, which allowed attaching the ways to the bedrock.[65]

The shoreline in Benicia that Turner selected for his shipyard was owned by Commodore John L. Eckley, an avid sailor. Turner partnered with his brother, Horatio, and with Eckley to open the shipyard.

Figure 41: Horatio Turner circa 1880 (left) and John L. Eckley circa 1875 (right) Source: Ancestry (Horatio) and Contra Costa History (Eckley).

John L. Eckley came to California in 1850 and spent several years as a land agent for Thomas O. Larkin in Sacramento. After spending a few years at Lake Tahoe, he moved to the San Francisco Bay area. He founded the small town of Eckley along the Carquinez Strait in the 1870s. He was one of the organizers of the San Francisco Yacht Club, and Turner had built him the yacht *Pearl* in 1876.

Originally called the Turner-Eckley shipyard, the yard was constructed along the Carquinez Strait shoreline at West 12th Street in Benicia. This included blocks 52, 53, 215 and 216. Blocks 215 and 216 extend into the Carquinez Strait. Horatio Turner and the Chapman family had property on two adjacent lots (lots 11 and 12 of block 52 respectively) within the bounds of the shipyard on the south side of K Street.[66]

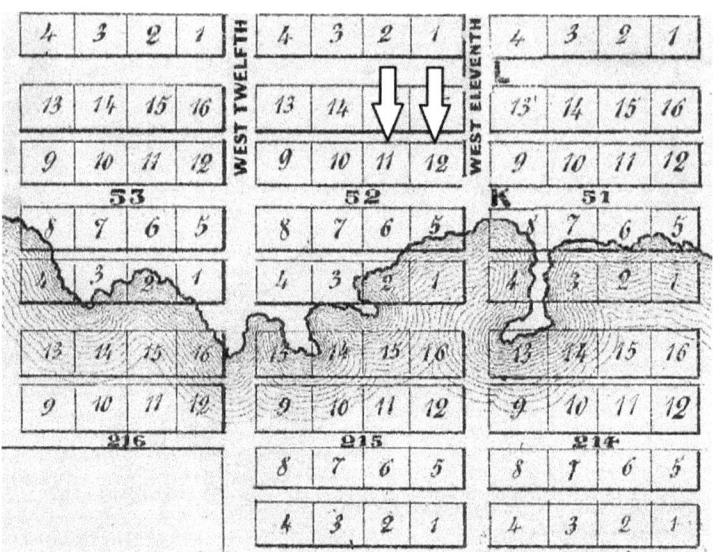

Figure 42: Turner shipyard blocks (52, 53, 215, 216) and Horatio Turner lot 11, and Chapman family lot 12 (arrows)
Source: City of Benicia Map of 1847, Benjamin W, Barlow.

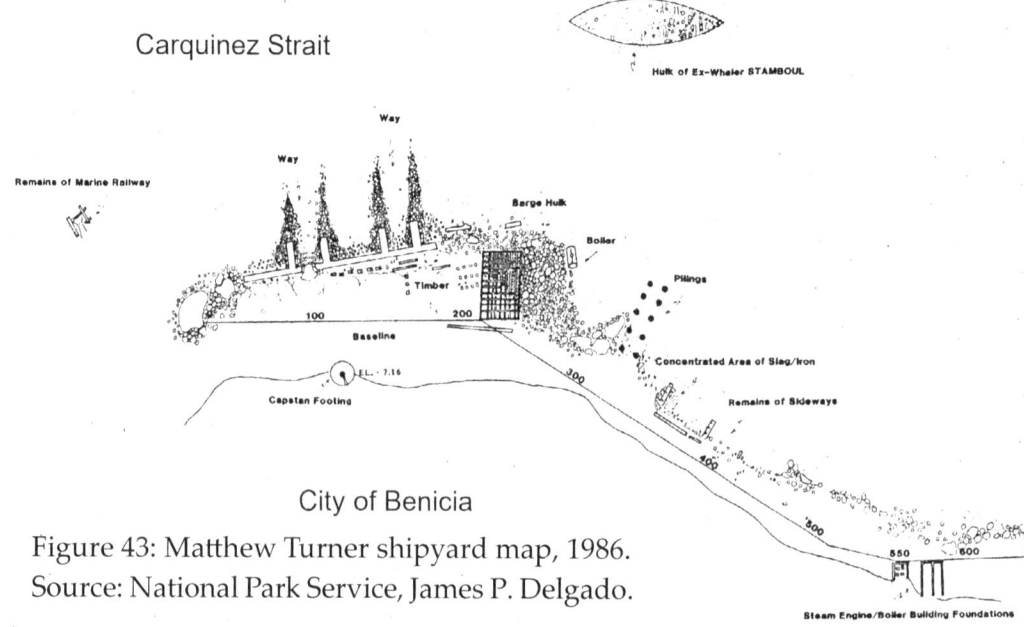

Figure 43: Matthew Turner shipyard map, 1986.
Source: National Park Service, James P. Delgado.

The shipyard was on a point that had a sloping 220-foot-long area for marine ways used to launch vessels was designed with concrete foundations cut into the sandstone, and a series of ways, and structures that support the ship under construction. A capstan, a vertical-axled rotating wench with cables used for pulling vessels onto the ways, was installed on the shore (see Figure 43).

There were several buildings at the shipyard. A sawmill used steam power to run the saws and other machinery needed to shape the timbers. The two specific pieces of equipment in the mill were band saws and a trunnel machine. The trunnel machine made wooden pegs from dry compressed timber so as to swell in its hole when moistened. Above the mill in the loft was a large where area where designing the ships and patterns of a ship were laid down full size on the floor, where molds and templates were made from them. In another area in the mill loft was an area to process oakum, a component in the caulking process to waterproof ships. Two men, sitting on stools and wearing aprons, would take the course fibrous oakum material soaked in oil and roll it up into long strips. Strips were set aside and another strip was started.[67] Other buildings included a forge and blacksmith shop located to the left of the mill, a privy, and other various sheds and buildings.

The typical cost of schooners in 1885 was between $5,500 and $11,000 each, and steamers were $20,000 each. Additional costs were added for internal gallery furnishings. There were between twenty-five to fifty workers at the shipyard at any given time. Every week they were paid by Mrs. Chapman in gold and silver coins as paper money was scarce.[68]

For the shipyard employees, there was a boarding house built at the shipyard. Also, the Erickson Hotel, a three-story building located across the road from the main gate to the shipyard, was available. There were small houses built nearby. Some lived in Vallejo or San Francisco and went home once a week.[69]

Figure 44: Erickson Hotel located across the street from the shipyard's main gate at West F Street and K Street, 1901.
Source: Museum of History Benicia.

The boarding house burned down on the night of October 1, 1895. All the employees managed to escape, but a few suffered severe burns on their hands and faces. A couple of buildings and a vessel in the shipyard also caught fire from the sparks, but the employees were able to extinguish them. The fire was suspected to be the work of an arsonist who was never identified.[70]

The first vessel built at the Turner and Eckley Benicia shipyard was the schooner *Amethyst*, launched Tuesday, July 22, 1883. The vessel, 72 ½ feet long and with a 74-ton capacity, was built for Captain Lewis Merrill of San Francisco.

Figure 45: Newspaper article announcing the launch of the first vessel, the schooner *Amethyst*, built in the Turner and Eckley shipyard in Benicia.
Source: *The Napa Register* Friday, July 27, 1883

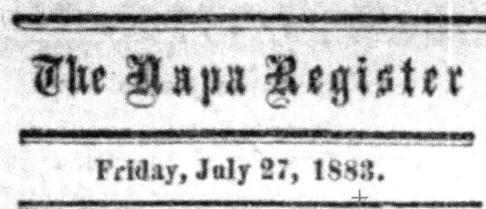

To celebrate the opening of the new Turner-Eckley shipyard in Benicia, the San Francisco Yacht Club organized a cruise of several yachts to Benicia at 1 P. M. Saturday, August 18th. Twenty yachts left San Francisco and entered the Carquinez Strait together in a "squadron" formation. A dance was held in one of the shipyard buildings, organized by Mrs. Eckley. In the evening, a moonlight cruise was held on the yachts.[71]

In January 1884, when correspondent M.J. Sanderson of the *San Francisco Call* visited the new Turner and Eckley yard, he described the marine ways to the west of the wharf as the largest in the country.

> *We noticed some thirty men around the yard. The principal work being done by Messrs. Turner and Eckley building the 401-ton rig Courtney Ford for San Francisco owners, which was launched on Wednesday last. The work in hand when we visited, besides finishing up the brig, was a steam launch, for use of the builders, 35 feet long, with 8 feet of beam. In the carpenter's shop, a cutter for the Mexican Government, 21 feet long, is being fitted up very handsomely. The people of Benicia are highly pleased with the coming of Messrs. Turner and Eckley among them, and on all hands, we heard earnest wishes for the success of their old enterprise in a new place.*

In 1888, there were about 80 men employed at Matthew Turner shipyard in Benicia.[72] There were a total of twelve vessels built that year.

Matthew continued to use the Fulton Iron Works for vessels requiring steam engines. When the Fulton Iron Works caught fire and burned down on October 19, 1887, and then Matthew switched to the Union Iron Works Company in San Francisco. As gasoline engines came of age, the Union Gas Engine Company was established in 1885 and was one of the very first manufacturers of gasoline engines of any kind in the United States. Matthew Turner first built gas auxiliary vessels in 1895.

Figure 46: Structures and timber at Matthew Turner shipyard, circa 1890.
Source: Museum of History Benicia/Don K. Oliver.

Figure 47: Inside Turner mold loft, A.E Chapman (right), 1890.
Source: The Hunt Family.

While Matthew Turner continued to live in San Francisco he managed both the Benicia shipyard and his San Francisco business. To get to Benicia, Turner and his crew would travel by train to Port Costa, board the *Gadder* or the *Poor Beggar* which were docked there, then sail across the Carquinez Strait to the shipyard.[73]

Figure 48: Matthew and Horatio Turner at the shipyard, circa 1895.
Source: The Hunt Family.

George Turner, Matthew and Horatio's father, was fascinated by the work of his sons in California, He traveled by train in July 1882 to visit them in San Francisco when he was 88 years old.[74] He made a voyage to Honolulu and back with Horatio. San Francisco, however, did not suit George Turner, and he returned to Geneva in May 1883, a refreshed man. But old age finally caught up with him on June 18, 1884.[75]

In 1885, Julian McAllister, Benicia Arsenal Commanding Officer, placed a proposal in the *Daily Alta California* for the construction of a steamer boat hull 60 feet long. The Arsenal's current steamer components (steam engine, boiler, shaft and propeller, etc.), were to be transferred into the new boat hull free of cost to the government. Matthew Turner got the contract and delivered finished the *John Rodgers* steamer on June 22.

Figure 49: Benicia Arsenal proposal for a boat hull.
Source: *Daily Alta California*, April 11, 1885.

Figure 50: Steamer *John Rodgers*, 1885.
Source: Museum of History Benicia.

In April 1887, Turner launched the *Thistle*, a whaleback steam tug. She was the first whaleback and most remarkable vessel ever constructed on the Pacific Coast. The whaleback had an unusual design, with a hull that continuously curved above the waterline from vertical to horizontal. She was designed to overcome the difficulty experienced by all small steamers on the northern bars and was completely housed over like the whalebacks of Captain McDougall of Duluth. She carried salmon out over the bars in and out of season, and the designer aimed to build a vessel that would not heed a breaking bar. Is was thought the whaleback would throw the sea like a duck. She had two propellers on one shaft, at stem and stern, and her deck was almost a semi-circle. The *Thistle* was 72 feet long and had one mast and cabin accommodations for eight persons. The vessel was built for R. D. Hume & Company and cost $13,000, and put into service on the Smith River in Northern California. The whalebacks were a success in the Great Lakes, but not on the Pacific Coast. The *Thistle* was converted to an ordinary type of steamer in 1897.[76]

Figure 51: Illustration of the whaleback vessel.
Source: *San Francisco Call*, August 23, 1891.

In January 1888, Turner built the stern-wheel steamer *Fruto* for the Freeman, Smith & Company. The *Fruto* was 429 tons with two decks and a length of 235 feet.

Figure 52: The stern-wheel steamer *Fruto*, circa 1900.
Source: San Francisco Maritime Historical Library.

In 1895, Matthew Turner bought the hulk of the whaling bark *Stamboul* for use as a work platform. Launched in 1843, the *Stamboul* was a 260-ton whaler measuring just over 106 feet in length. It was used in the Boston trade, shipping ice cut from

Wenham Lake, just north of Boston, and shipping goods to Calcutta, the Caribbean, and South America. The *Stamboul* entered into a new trade after the Civil War. In 1866, the ship was used for whaling in the Atlantic and, later, in the Indian Ocean. The discovery of new whaling grounds in the Sea of Cortez brought the *Stamboul* to the Pacific. In 1884, the *Stamboul* was sold to James McKenna of San Francisco. Becoming an outdated relic, her last voyage was in 1894. The *Stamboul* languished in the backwaters of the San Francisco Bay, awaiting her eventual breaking up.[77]

Figure 53: The whaler *Stamboul*, 1880s.
Source: The Hunt Family.

The Turner shipyard purchased the *Stamboul*, striped of her useable fittings, and moved the vessel to the shipyard for use as a work platform.[78] The *Stamboul* hulk was positioned parallel to the shore, 120 yards offshore, and to the west of the ways. She was stabilized with gravel and rock in her hold, and a pair of shear poles were erected on her main deck aft. A pier was built from shore out to the *Stamboul* with an "L" shape forming a permanent platform on the starboard side of the ship. The *Stamboul* was used to build masts for ships under construction positioned alongside the platform.

The *Stamboul* still rests in the mud offshore from Turner's shipyard site to this day. The location is shown in the Matthew Turner shipyard map, Figure 43.

Figure 54: View of the shipyard with the *Stamboul* shown (at a right angle to the pier). circa 1902.
Source: The Hunt Family.

Figure 55: Matthew Turner shipyard with 4-masted schooner *Amaranth* at the dock, circa 1902. The *Stamboul* can be seen at a right angle to the ship.
Source: Museum of History Benicia.

In October 1892, the largest ship built at the Benicia shipyard, the brigantine *Geneva*, was launched. She was a two-masted half-brigantine of actually 495.66 tons and 150 feet long at this time.

Figure 56: The largest ship built at the Benicia shipyard, the *Geneva*. Source: *San Francisco Call*, October 6, 1892.

Between May and November of 1893, the country faced a severe financial panic. This led to a run on currency, the closure of banks, and businesses and manufacturers being unable to operate due to the lack of funds to pay workers or purchase raw materials. As a consequence, only five vessels were built at the Matthew Turner shipyard during that period.

In 1894, Turner received a contract to build a dry dock for the California Drydock Company in San Francisco. The dry dock had a 301-foot length and was large enough to accommodate any vessel that would come to the port of San Francisco of average tonnage. Over 170 men, including 106 carpenters, worked on this dry dock.[79] The drydock was completed in March 1895. The drydock weighed 2,700 tons.

Figure 57: Report of the contract for the drydock .
Source: *San Francisco Call*, June 28, 1894.

Figure 58: The floating drydock pictured under construction at the Turner Shipyard, 1894.
The Erickson Hotel can be seen in the background on the left.
Source: Museum of History Benicia.

Figure 59: The floating drydock is completed at the Turner Shipyard, 1895. To gauge the size, note the man on the right side of the drydock.
Source: Museum of History Benicia.

Chapter Nine
The Brigantine *Galilee*

The *Galilee* was a half-brigantine, 132.5 feet long and with a 354-ton capacity, designed and built by Matthew Turner, and launched in February 1891. She began her career on the packet line between San Francisco and Tahiti carrying freight, passengers, and French and US mail. On her maiden voyage, she set a record of 19 days from San Francisco to Tahiti and 22 ½ days on return, a straight windward haul.[80]

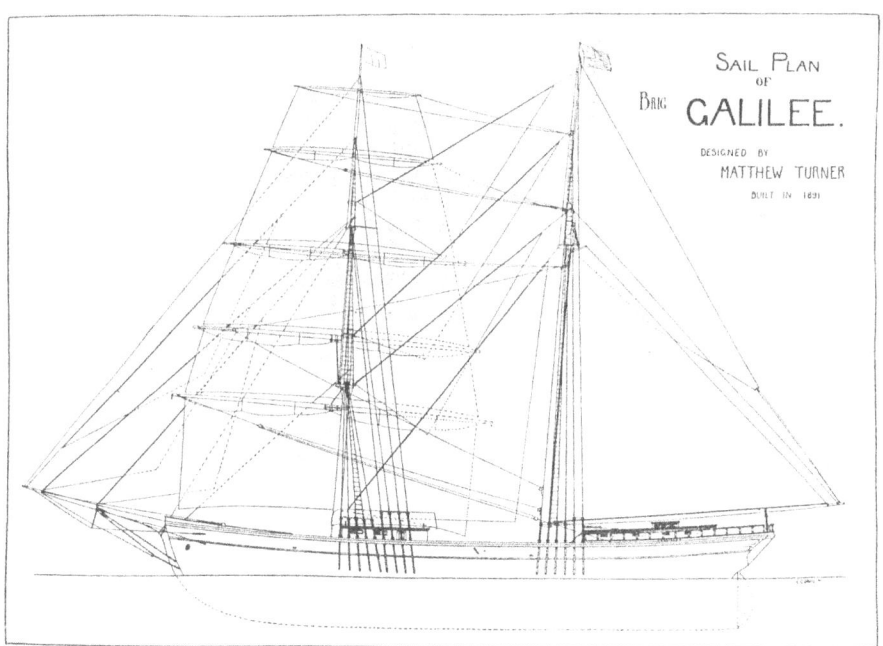

Figure 60: *Galilee* half-brigantine sail plan.
Source: drawn by C. C. Davis.

Figure 61: The *Galilee*, circa 1895.
Source: Museum of History Benicia.

The design of the *Galilee* was a half-brigantine, meaning it was square-rigged on the foremast, and rigged fore-and-aft, parallel to the ship's side, on the main mast. She was the last of the three speedy packet vessels of Matthew Turner's Tahiti Packet Line, which sailed from San Francisco to Papeete between 1891 and 1896. Not simply cargo carriers, they were also designed for passengers and light freight such as mail and perishable fruits. *Galilee* set two records on her maiden voyage.[81]

Figure 62: Pictured is the keel of the *Galilee* being carved at the shipyard, 1890.
Horatio Turner is standing behind the keel on the left.
Source: The Hunt Family.

The *Galilee* was launched in February 1891. Captain Turner and a host of friends enjoyed the event.

Figure 63: Newspaper excerpt regarding the launch of the *Galilee*.
Source: *San Francisco Call*, February 16, 1891.

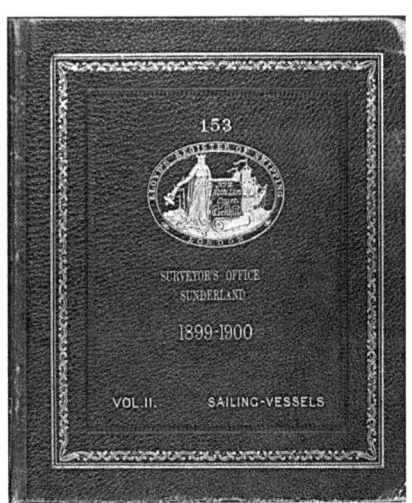

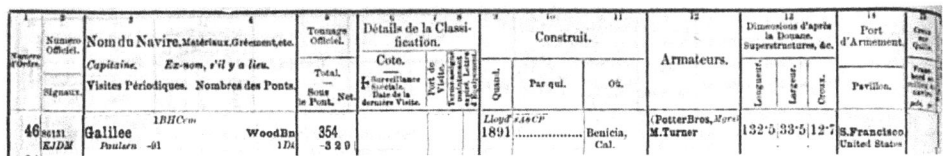

Figure 64: *Galilee* listed in *Lloyd's Register*.
Source: *Lloyd's Register of Shipping, Vol II, Sailing Vessels, 1899-1900*.

Figure 65: Matthew Turner standing on the deck of the *Galilee* in 1905.
Source: San Francisco Maritime Historical Library.

The Captain's quarters were located inside at the stern of the ship. The *Galilee* was exquisitely furnished with a fireplace, an organ, and sleeping quarters with a window.

Figure 66: Captain's quarters on the *Galilee* complete with fireplace.
Source: The Hunt Family.

Figure 67: Another view of the Captain's quarters on the *Galilee*.
Source: The Hunt Family.

Figure 68: Captain's quarters on the *Galilee* with organ.
Source: San Francisco Maritime National Historical Library.

Figure 69: Captain's sleeping quarters on the *Galilee*.
Source: San Francisco Maritime National Historical Library.

In 1905, the *Galilee* was chartered by the Carnegie Institution's Department of Terrestrial Magnetism and converted into a magnetic observatory. She was used to make observations of the Earth's magnetic field on three cruises over a period of three years from 1905 to 1908 in the Pacific Ocean.

The Department of Terrestrial Magnetism was founded by Louis Agricola Bauer in 1904, with Bauer as its first director. He recognized that the magnetic field over the oceans was not surveyed and looked for a suitable vessel to make magnetic observations. In 1905, the *Galilee* was chartered by the Carnegie Institution's Department of Terrestrial Magnetism to be converted into a magnetic observatory. The amount of magnetic materials on the ship was reduced to a minimum. The steel rigging was replaced by hemp ropes and a new observation bridge was constructed to lift the observation point on which sensitive instruments were mounted as far as possible above the remaining iron parts of the ship, principally bolts in the vessel's sides. Additional cabin space was also provided to accommodate the scientists.

Figure 70: *Galilee* observation bridge, between the two masts.
Note the man climbing aloft using the rope ladder.
Source: Museum of History Benicia.

Although the converted *Galilee* had magnetic constants lower than any equivalent ship at the time, corrections were still required to take account of the remaining magnetic material. These corrections were measured using a procedure known as 'swinging ship' in which the *Galilee* was held aligned towards the north, observations of the magnetic field were noted and the ship was turned progressively at 15° intervals (or as many as could be obtained given the prevailing conditions) using the right rudder, followed by a similar set using the left rudder. As the ship's own magnetic field changed with time, because of induction effects on the soft iron parts of the ship, this procedure had to be repeated as often as possible, generally in the harbor or occasionally at sea if the conditions were calm enough.

On August 5, 1905, the *Galilee* left San Francisco on a shakedown cruise. During this week-long cruise, the various instruments and procedures were tested under the supervision of the Director. Bauer also completed the training of the observers.

Then, Cruise I, began on September 1, 1905, with the *Galilee* sailing to Honolulu, arriving on September 16. Following a further swing and land observations at the Honolulu Magnetic Observatory, the ship sailed to Fanning Island, arriving on October 10. From there the *Galilee* returned to Honolulu, taking a course farther to the west.

The ship then sailed to the north of the Hawaiian Islands before returning to San Diego, arriving at her home port on December 9. A final set of swings and shore observations were made at San Diego, finishing on December 18. A distance of 10,571 nautical miles was covered on the first cruise. The commander was J. F. Pratt, taken temporarily into the employ of the Department of Terrestrial Magnetism. J.P Ault, the future commander of the *Carnegie*, was one of the magnetic observers.[82]

Cruise II, carried out under the supervision of J. F. Pratt, began on March 2, 1906, heading straight to Fanning Island. The cruise continued to Pago Pago on Tutuila, part of the Samoan islands, where neither swings nor shore observations proved possible. From Pago, the ship continued to Apia, where land observations were made at the German Geophysical Laboratory there, although again no swing was possible. The *Galilee* then sailed for Suva in the Fiji Islands, where the ship was successfully swung and more shore observations were carried out. The next part of the cruise included stops at the Marshall Islands and Guam before arriving at Yokohama in Japan on August 13.

While in the harbor at Yokohama, the ship was caught by a typhoon in which she dragged her anchors and sank. Fortunately, the damage was relatively slight. She was recovered and put in dry-dock where repairs were carried out. From Japan the *Galilee* returned to San Diego, arriving on October 19, having covered 16,286 nautical miles.[83]

Cruise III began on December 22, 1906, when the *Galilee* set out from San Diego. The first port of call was Nuku Hiva in the Marquesas Islands, but the ship soon moved on to Tahiti, where shore observations and swings could be carried out. The next stop was Apia, where observations were again made at the geophysical observatory. On March 14, 1907, the *Galilee* moved on to Yap Island and from there to Shanghai, arriving on May 8. Shore observations were made at the Zikawei Observatory, but the ship was swung in the mouth of the Yangtze River as the large tidal variation prevented this upriver at Shanghai.

The next intended stop was Midway Island, but stormy weather made this impossible and prevented most magnetic observations. The *Galilee* reached Sitka in Alaska on July 14, having covered 5,507 nautical miles in 41 days, an average of about 134 miles per day. New instruments were added, including an electric potential gradient and the current sensor for making atmospheric-electric observations. At Sitka, Paul H. Dike joined the cruise's scientific staff to perform the observations. On August 10, the ship set off once more, heading for Honolulu, which she reached on August 28. After being overhauled and refitted, the *Galilee* sailed for Jaluit on the Marshall Islands, where a further set of readings were taken for comparison with those taken in 1907.

The ship then set sail on November 5, aiming for Port Lyttelton in New Zealand. However, on November 11, the *Galilee* still at Jaluit, becalmed and in danger of being stranded on a reef, and had to be towed off by a German mail steamer. The lack of an auxiliary power source, which had caused this problem, also made the trip to New Zealand extremely difficult as the winds and currents drove her towards the New Hebrides Islands. On arrival at Port Lyttleton, the ship was further delayed as Ernest Shackleton was about to depart from that port on the Nimrod Expedition to Antarctica.

Figure 71: The *Galilee* at drydock at Lyttelton, New Zealand, undergoing repairs, December 1907.
Source: San Francisco Maritime National Historical Library.

By January 17, 1908, the necessary observations having been made, the *Galilee* set sail due east. Eventually turning northeast, she arrived in Callao, Peru on March 10. The ship had sustained some damage to her rudder due to very strong winds encountered during early February, which took two weeks to repair. She sailed from Callao on April 5 heading just north of west, south of the Galapagos Islands, before turning north and then northwest, following roughly parallel to the coast. Finally, the *Galilee* headed northeast to San Francisco, arriving on May 21, 1908. Following a final set of swings and shore observations, the vessel was returned to its owners on June 5, 1908. The final cruise covered a distance of 36,977 nautical miles, giving a total distance for the period of her charter to the Department of Terrestrial Magnetism as 63,834 nautical miles.[84]

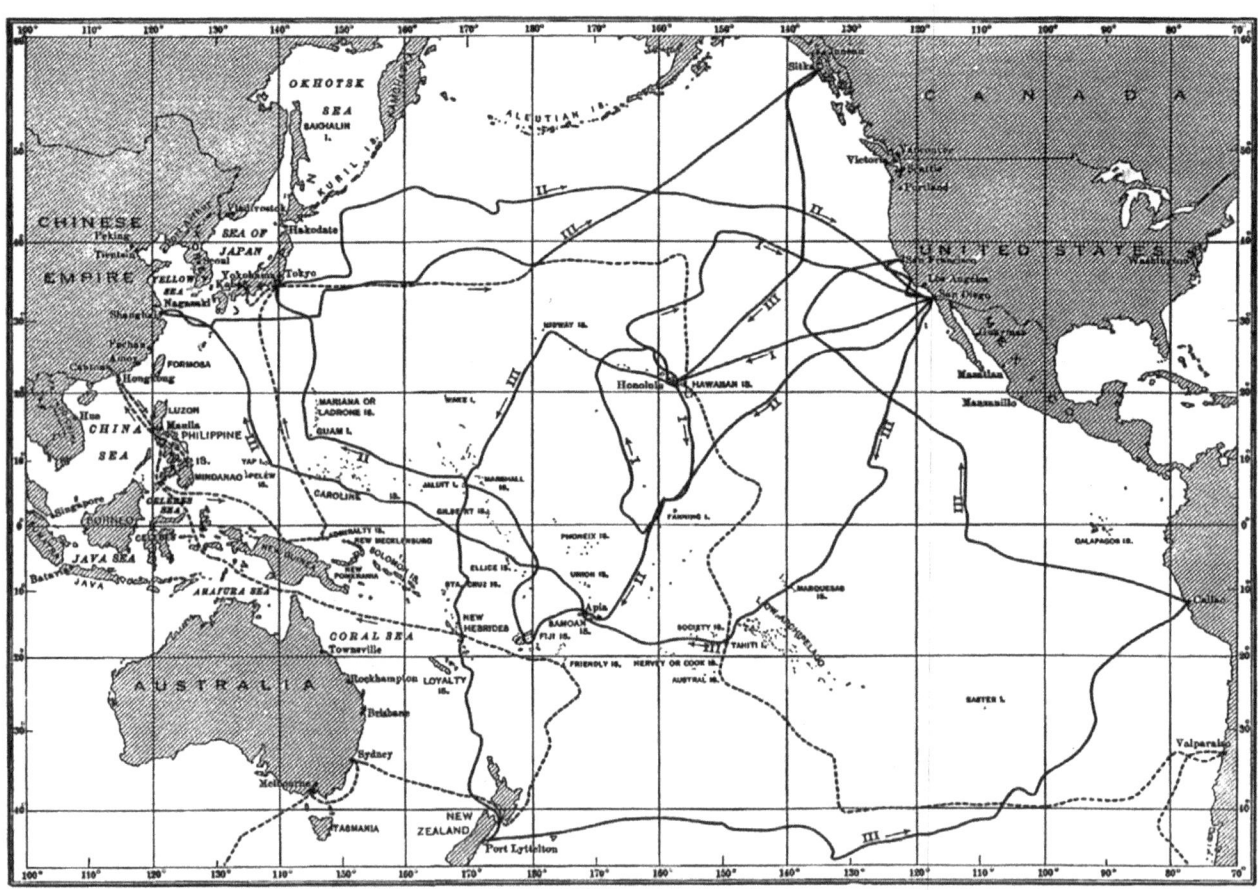

Figure 72: Map showing the three cruises of the *Galilee*.
Source: *Ocean Magnetic Observations, Plate 6*, 1905-1908, by Louis A. Bauer.

Figure 73: Dr. Louis A. Bauer, Director of the Carnegie Institution's Department of Terrestrial Magnetism, makes magnetic observations on board the *Galilee* in 1905.
Source: Museum of History Benicia.

Figure 74: Members of the *Galilee* crew using sextants to determine the position of their vessel.
Note the two men on the observation deck (center).
Source: Museum of History Benicia.

Figure 75: The scientific party seated at dinner on board the *Galilee* during her third cruise in 1907, from left to right, included P.H. Dike, Commander D.C. Sowers, W.J. Peters (Commander), and G. Peterson.
Source: Archives of the Department of Terrestrial Magnetism, Carnegie Institute of Washington, D. C.

Figure 76: The *Galilee* during "Cruise III" from San Diego on December 22, 1906 to San Francisco on May 21, 1908.
Source: Museum of History Benicia.

Figure 77: The *Galilee* in San Diego, California,
Dressed for Washington's Birthday celebrations, February 1906.
Source: Museum of History Benicia.

By the early 1900s, steamships were beginning to compete with the great sailing ships of the previous century, but *Galilee's* reputation for speed kept her in service well into the steam era. In 1911, the *Galilee* was sold to the Union Fish Company of San Francisco and was converted to a three-masted schooner in 1913 to be used in the Alaska Fishing Industry. For sixteen years the *Galilee* was used to fish for codfish, then in 1929, she was used by the tuna industry.

In 1933, the *Galilee* was beached in Richardson Bay Sausalito in what later became known as "Galilee Harbor." She operated as a houseboat and an office for 42 more years. In 1975, her stern was salvaged and restored. and was put on display at Fort Mason, San Francisco.

Figure 78: The *Galilee* stern at Fort Mason, San Francisco, 2024.
Source: Photograph by author.

Figure 79: The *Galilee* stern with the ship name faintly visible with "San Francisco" beneath, 2024.
Source: Photograph by author.

In 1987, her bow was removed and brought to Benicia and remained at the City Corporation Yard on East Second Street until it was moved to the Museum of History Benicia in February 1994.

Figure 80: The *Galilee* in Sausalito mud flats, circa 1970.
The name *Galilee* is visible along the top of the deck.
Source: San Francisco Maritime National Historical Library.

Figure 81: Museum of History Benicia volunteers Ted Anderson, Jim Phelan, Tom Hosley, Peter Bray, Ron Rice, Dick Lubin, and Vernon Gross, working on *Galilee* bow enclosure. 1995.
Source: Museum of History Benicia.

Figure 82: The *Galilee* bow at the Museum of History Benicia, 2024.
Source: Photograph by author.

Chapter Ten
Matthew Turner's Later Years

Matthew never did live in Benicia. He resided in San Francisco and managed his business from his office at 40 California Street. He traveled every week to Benicia with the payroll (gold coins) and to consult with his brother Horatio on the operation of the yard.[85] He hired Charlie Chapman as a draftsman, and Charlie went on as a designer, ship architect, and manager of the shipyard when Turner retired. Nelson Andrews, the husband of Eva Rundle, learned the shipbuilding business and became a bookkeeper and clerk in San Francisco at the California Street offices of M. Turner and Company.[86] He took over the business with his friend and partner, Captain Ed Bowes, when Turner retired.[87]

Matthew was equally famous for building fast sailing yachts. He was a long-time member of the San Francisco Yacht Club and a Charter member of the Vallejo Yacht Club. Some of the famous prize-winning yachts that he built were the *Nellie*, the *Chispa*, the *Jessie*, the *Truant*, the *Lurline* (the yacht), and the *Ramona*. He also built ten sloops which were used in races. The most famous were the *Colorado*, the *Poor Beggar*, the *Gadder*, and the *Gertrude*. He never became Commodore of the club but he held other offices including Measurer. The Measurer checked each boat's length before a regatta to determine if it required a handicap.

The *Gadder* was Turner's entry in the San Francisco Perpetual Challenge Trophy race of 1899 and 1900. Turner was one of the original contestants in this race series since 1895. The *Gadder* was sailed by Captain McCarthy in the 1899 race against the *Truant* of the Corinthian Yacht Club and won by one minute fifty-eight seconds. In 1900 Commander A.E. Chapman skippered the *Gadder* against the *Aeolus* of the Corinthian Yacht Club and lost by sixteen minutes. These yachts continued to participate in the Perpetual Cup regattas in the early 1900s.

Figure 83: Perpetual Cup race in circa 1900. Pictured are the yachts *Truant* (left), the *Emma* (center) and the *Mignon* (right).
Source: The Hunt Family

The *Truant* and the *Mignon* (owned by John W. Steward and George W. Phillips of Marysville) were in the 30-foot class and the *Emma* was in the 35-foot class.

One of the smallest yachts Turner built was the *Villain*. This little 30-foot 2-masted yacht was built in 1897 and participated in the San Francisco Bay races.

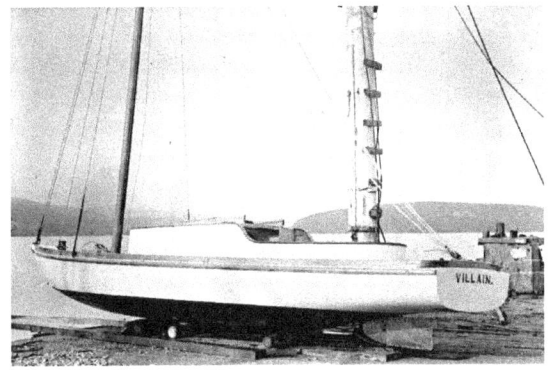

Figure 84: The Yacht *Villain*, 1897.
Source: Museum of History Benicia.

Captain Turner, being a master sailor, rarely makes errors. But in January 1898, the 72-year-old captain had a mishap that caused minor damage to his schooner *Hercules*. When returning from the trail run Turner did not slow down quickly enough and crashed into the bark *Roderick Dhu* at the wharf in San Francisco causing damage to the vessel's jib-boom.

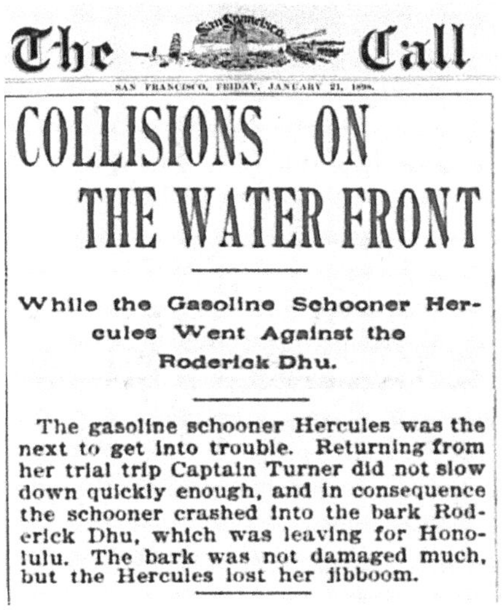

The Call

SAN FRANCISCO, FRIDAY, JANUARY 21, 1898.

COLLISIONS ON THE WATER FRONT

While the Gasoline Schooner Hercules Went Against the Roderick Dhu.

The gasoline schooner Hercules was the next to get into trouble. Returning from her trial trip Captain Turner did not slow down quickly enough, and in consequence the schooner crashed into the bark Roderick Dhu, which was leaving for Honolulu. The bark was not damaged much, but the Hercules lost her jibboom.

Figure 85: Newspaper article on Captain Turner's mishap.
Source: *San Francisco Call*, January 21, 1898.

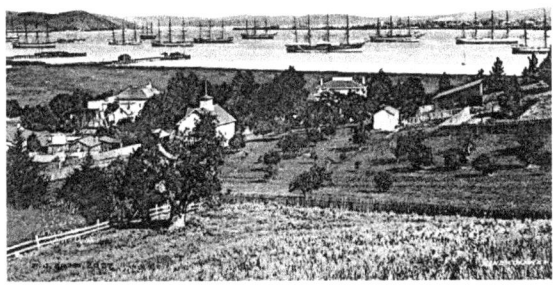

Figure 86: View of ships in Carquinez Strait from Martinez looking towards Benicia.
Source: Frank Stumm postcard, circa 1900.

Matthew Turner included his family when it came time to christen his vessels, The schooner *Rosamond* was christened by Charlotte Chapman in 1900, the *Solano* was christened by his grandson Adrien Rundle Chapman in 1901 at age 11, and the schooner *Matthew Turner* was christened by his granddaughter Eva in 1902 at age 13.[88]

CHRISTENING THE ROSAMOND, TO WITNESS WHOSE LAUNCHING THE SYBIL AND CROWLEY RACED.

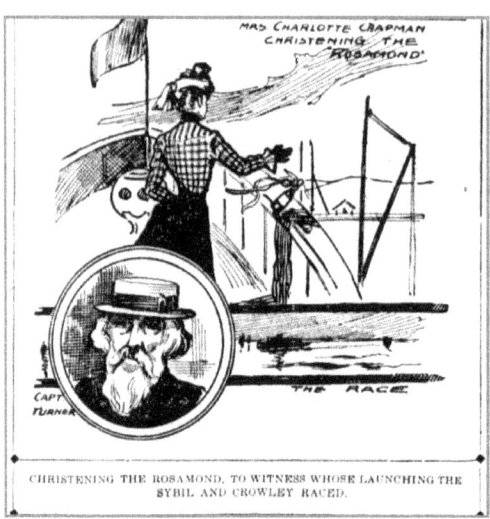

Figure 87: Mrs. Charlotte Chapman christening the *Rosamond,* named after the four-year-old daughter of F. M. Swauzy, the managing owner. Source: *San Francisco Examiner,* May 20, 1900.

THE SAN FRANCISCO CALL, FRIDAY, MARCH 8, 1901.

SCHOONER LAUNCHED AT BENICIA YARDS

One Thousand Spectators Witness the Christening of the Solano.

BENICIA, March 7.—A four-masted schooner 190 feet long, 40 foot beam and 14 feet 6 inches depth of hold was successfully launched from Captain Turner's shipyards here this afternoon. She was christened The Solano, in honor of the County in which she was built. Master Chapman, a young son of A. E. Chapman, manager of the yard, and grandson of Captain Turner, broke the bottle of wine across her bows. Through the efforts of Supervisor Crooks of this city the County Board presented the vessel with a complete code of signal flags.

Fully 1000 spectators witnessed the launching and nearly 100, including the members of the famous Benicia Juvenile band, were on deck when the word was given and the vessel slipped out into the bay.

The Solano will be ready for duty in about three weeks and her first voyage will be to Alaska. She is chartered by the Alaska Salmon Packing Company. Captain Rosich is to be in command.

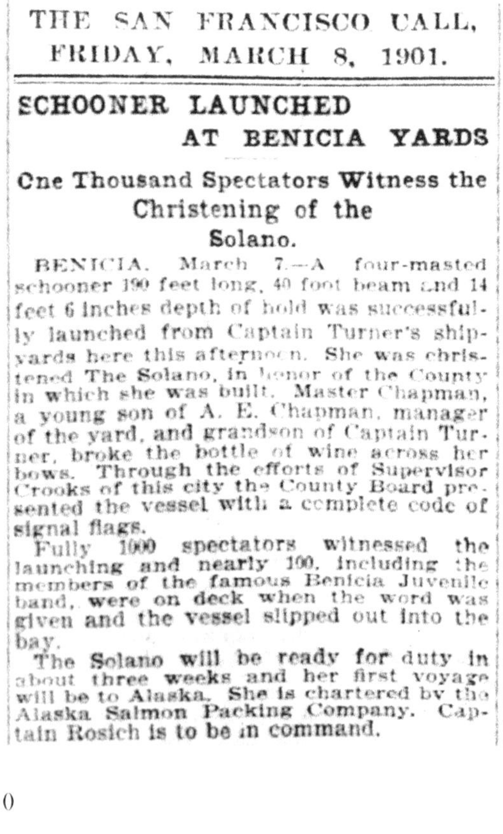

Figure 88: Newspaper excerpt of the christening of the schooner *Solano* in which 1,000 spectators attended. Source: *San Francisco Call.* March 8, 1901.

Figure 89: The 4-masted *Solano* under construction, 1901.
Source: Museum of History Benicia.

When Turner was asked why he hadn't recently named a ship after himself, he replied that he intended to, but not until he could personally pick out every stick of material and then closely superintend the construction of the craft to bear his name. In 1902 the time came when he could do this and the new schooner *Matthew Turner* was the result. She is one of the trimmest crafts in port, and Turner says "She is just as good as she looks."[89]

Figure 90: The *Matthew Turner*, a 4-masted schooner, 185 feet long, 816-ton capacity.
Source: Museum of History Benicia.

Figure 91: Newspaper excerpt about the building of the *Matthew Turner* schooner.
Source: *San Francisco Call*, March 18, 1902.

On August 7, 1902, the *Matthew Turner*, docked at the Howard Street wharf in San Francisco, scheduled to sail to Eureka to load lumber for delivery to Australia. Tommy Ryan, a small boy living nearby at 1731 Harrison Street, stowed away on the *Matthew Turner*. A few minutes after the vessel left the wharf, young Ryan's mother appeared and inquired anxiously about the boat and her boy. A telegram was sent to Eureka and when the *Matthew Turner* arrived, Tommy, who by that time had had all the sailing he wanted, was shipped home to his mother.

Figure 92: Stowed Away on *Matthew Turner*.
Source: *San Francisco Call*, August 8, 1902.

The Matthew Turner Shipyard was not only involved in shipbuilding but also offered repair services for ships and vessels. In 1901, the shipyard upgraded its machinery for construction, including the addition of boring and riveting machines. As a result, they were able to perform modern and up-to-date work on short notice.[90]

Pictured below is the schooner *White Wings* at the Benicia shipyard for repairs. The yacht collided with the schooner *Alliance* at night on April 3, 1897, near Vallejo.

Figure 93: The schooner *White Wings* awaiting repair at the Benicia shipyard, 1897.
Source: Museum of History Benicia.

In 1901, the stern-wheel steamer *Vallette* was built at the Benicia shipyard by W. D. Delaney for the Farmer's Transportation Agency. She was used for the Sacramento grain trade from San Francisco to Colusa. The steamer carried only grain, not passengers. For years, the Colusa farmers have protested the high transportation rates charged by the railroads. Three additional similar steamers were planned to be built for the Farmer's Transportation Agency.[91]

In May 1905 the Norwegian ships *Victoria* and *Salamis* were wrecked at Malden Island in the South Pacific during a gale on May 19. The vessels were a total loss. The crews had saved themselves but were stranded on the island for several weeks. The schooner *Matthew Turner*, commanded by Captain Carl Jensen, discovered the unfortunate crew on June 11 and took them aboard.

In acknowledgment of this event, the King of Norway sent Matthew Turner a silver coffee server and a set of goblets. Captain Carl Jensen received a silver cup with the Norwegian coat of arms and flag, underneath were the words: "For heroic deed in rescuing the crews of the two Norwegian vessels, Victoria and Salamis, stranded on Malden Island in 1905."

Figure 94: Newspaper article on the rescue of Norwegian crews.
Source: *San Francisco Call*, July 6, 1905.

Figure 95: Newspaper Norwegian Government gift to Captain Carl Jensen.
Source: *San Pedro News*, November 20, 1906.

San Pedro Daily News

TUESDAY, NOVEMBER 20, 1906.

San Francisco, Nov. 20.—Captain Matthew Turner, shipbuilder and ship owner, has been honored by the Norwegian Government, which presented him with a silver coffee set. This gift was in acknowledgement of the services performed by the schooner bearing his name and owned by him, which some eighteen months ago rescued the crews of the Norwegian ships Victor and Salamis, which were wrecked on Malden Island, in the South Pacific. Captain Carl Jensen, who was in command of the Turner at the time, was given a handsome silver goblet.

Figure 96: Horatio Turner and his wife, Mary Turner, on the steps of their home on West K Street, Benicia. Circa 1890s.
Source: The Hunt Family.

Figure 97: Home of Adrien E. "Charlie" Chapman and Charlotte "Dolly" Chapman on West K Street, Benicia in 1893.
Source: The Hunt Family.

Figure 98: Ashbeline M. Turner (center) with daughters Eva T. Nelson (left) and Charlotte "Dolly" Chapman (right), circa 1900.
Source: FamilySearch.org.

One of Charlotte Chapman's daughters was Eva, and Matthew was looked on as a grandfather. She lived with Ashbeline, her grandmother, and Matthew in San Francisco at an early age. She was very close to her grandparents.

Figure 99: Eva with Ashbeline and Matthew, 1892.
Source: The Hunt Family.

At night, Eva would crawl into bed with Matthew and he would read to her. He started with the *Brownie Books*, then graduated up to Kipling, *Alice in Wonderland*, and animal books.[92] In a letter dated December 8, 1890, from Matthew addressed to "Baby Chapman" he writes that he has "received a communication from Santa Claus," and "reports of your conduct are good." A doll is mentioned as just one of several possible Christmas gifts.[93]

When Eva was 10 years old, she went to an elementary school in San Francisco. Every Sunday, Matthew would take her on walks along the Embarcadero, which was a boardwalk at that time, to see the ships. Eva loved to admire the bowsprits and figureheads on the bigger ships. As they walked, Matthew would tell her about each ship, including the name of the captain and some of its history.[94]

Eva and her grandmother used to travel from San Francisco to the Benicia shipyard. They took a train from San Francisco to Port Costa, where a yacht from the shipyard would meet them. To reach the shore, they had to go through a series of saloons, as there were no openings between them. They were escorted by sailors to the yacht so that their long dresses would not get wet. They saw several saloons had pig pens under the wharves. When the tide came in, it would wash out the pig pens and keep them sanitary. The yacht would take them across the Carquinez Strait to the Benicia shipyard.[95]

Eva and her grandmother would spend the summers at the cabins near the shipyard in Benicia. She would sometimes bring her school girl friends to stay a week or two.[96]

Figure 100: Eva and Ashbeline at a cabin in Benicia, circa 1899.
Source: The Hunt Family.

For a short time, Eva attended the West End Grammar School, a one-room school located at West Sixth and K Streets in Benicia. The school had three grades and was taught by Mary Farmar. The school served the children on the west end of town before they transferred to the big school downtown.[97]

In 1906, Eva and her family, which included her mother, brother, and sister, had to stay at the Anderson Hotel in town during winter. The road near their home was too muddy to walk or ride a horse through, so they decided to stay at the hotel. The hotel provided them with a comfortable room and served meals. During their stay, they got to know the townspeople, as there were only working men out by the shipyard. Eva's brother, Rundle, graduated from Benicia High School in 1910, where he had attended.

Figure 101: Benicia High School students, 1907. Rundle Chapman is at the bottom left.
Source: Museum of History Benicia.

Matthew Turner's stepdaughters, Charlotte Jane Rundle and Eva Turner Rundle, were educated at the Young Ladies Seminar in Benicia by Turner's aunt, Mary Atkins Lynch from 1880 to 1881.

In 1889, Turner built a little sloop, the *Molly Woggin*, which he used for racing and to travel to his Benicia shipyard.

Figure 102: Newspaper article about Turner's sloop *Molly Woggin*.
Source: The Sausalito News, June 21, 1889.

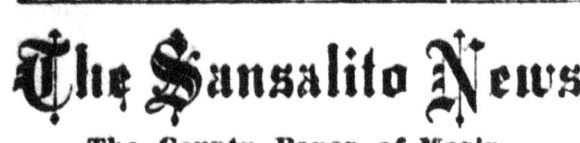

The *Molly Woggon*, Captain Turner's little sloop from Benicia, came down to the San Francisco Yacht Club opening last Saturday. She has never been beaten by a boat of her size.

The Morning Call.

SAN FRANCISCO, SUNDAY MORNING, MAY 28, 1893.

THEY SKIM THE SALT SEA WAVE.

Something About Our Fast-Racing Yachts.

Perhaps the fastest "all-round" schooner yacht we ever had here was the Nellie, built by Captain Matthew Turner. She was doubtless his masterpiece in centerboard craft, as the present Jessie is of the keel type. In the days of the Nellie, when she was owned by Hyde Bowie, and then by Mervyn Donahue, and sailed by Frank Murphy, she "carried the broom" in San Francisco Bay. She has gone down the south coast now, pretty well used up from carrying sail hard and being pressed beyond her powers. Although built as a centerboard boat with light frame and inside ballast, she was, to meet modern ideas, finally loaded with lead outside her keel. She sailed better with this, it is true, but it soon used her up, and she was sold for a nominal sum as having been strained too much for further racing contests.

The Chispa, Con O'Connor and Fleur de Lis, which were in her class, and the Aggie, which was larger, tried time and again to beat the Nellie, but without avail. Commodore Gutte of the Chispa was sure that in a strong breeze his favorite could win, and after several minor contests in annual regattas a match was made between the two fliers, Chispa and Nellie, in which the latter won.

THE SCHOONER NELLIE.

Figure 103: Newspaper excerpt about Matthew Turner's yachts, *Nellie* and *Chispa*.
Source: *San Francisco Call*, May 28, 1893.

Figure 104: Newspaper illustration about the launching of the schooner *Matthew Turner*.
Source: *San Francisco Call*, August 7, 1902.

After retiring from the sea, Horatio Turner settled in an "Old People's Home" located in the San Francisco area. In September 1907, a fire broke out in the home, and the veteran captain, who had previously fought many fires at sea, led the charge. Along with two other men in their 80s, he retrieved the emergency hoses and crawled under the smoke to reach the engine room where the fire had started. When the firefighters arrived, they found Horatio Turner pouring water on the blaze. This act of bravery was documented in the San Francisco Chronicle.[98]

In 1903, Matthew Turner suffered a stroke due to his advancing age and the stress of business affairs. Unfortunately, the stroke affected his speech, forcing him to retire from shipbuilding permanently. Despite this setback, he continued to enjoy sailing. Along with Ashbeline and Eva, he moved to 1436 Spruce Street in Berkeley and spent the rest of his life there.

The last ship built under the direction of Matthew Turner at the Benicia shipyard was the *St. Michael*, a 2-masted gas schooner, launched in October 1904.

Figure 105: *St. Michael* schooner, last vessel built at the Turner Shipyard in Benicia.
Source: *San Francisco Call*, October 24, 1904.

The Great San Francisco earthquake and fire of 1906 destroyed Matthew Turner's office in the city. Matthew commissioned four of his ships, paid for by his retirement funds, to help the city with rescue and salvage operations, and to help supply what was needed for the desperate people.[99]

In 1906, Matthew Turner contracted with the Bendixsen Shipyard at Fairhaven in Humboldt Bay, to build a ship for him, the steam schooner *Hoquiam*. Due to the earthquake, he took advantage of the lower-cost Mendocino lumber and avoided the very high freight charges predominant in the Bay Area.[100] The *Hoquiam*, a three-masted schooner, 181 feet in length, 641 tons, fitted with passenger accommodations. She was launched on September 1, 1906, and the hull was loaded with lumber and towed to San Francisco, where her engines were installed by the United Engineering Company. She serviced the lumber runs between the California coast and Hoquiam, Washington for several years.[101]

Figure 106: Article announcing the building of the *Hoquiam* for Matthew Turner at the Bendixsen Shipyard.
Source: *The Humboldt Times*, October 28, 1906.

ANOTHER BOAT TO BE BUILT HERE

A new steam schooner is to be built by the Bendixsen Shipbuilding Company of Eureka, for Matthew Turner of this city. The new coasting vessel will have a capacity of about 800,000 feet of lumber. The steam schooner Hoquiam, which was recently built for the same party, will be placed on the ways tomorrow to have her propeller and shaft installed.—San Francisco Examiner.

When Turner stepped down as head of the Benicia yard in 1904, the *San Francisco Chronicle* praised him for his shipbuilding successes, "Some of the best sailers that ever spread their canvas on the Pacific are the product of his skill."

On February 10, 1909, Turner died at his home in Berkeley, California, at the age of 83. He was survived by a widow, Ashbeline M. Turner of Berkeley; two sisters, Mrs. Phedora T. Jones of Geneva, Ohio, and Mrs. Stella P. Riordan of Chicago, and two nephews, Captain Louis H. Turner and Henry P. Gray (Ada's son) of San Francisco. Ashbeline died in 1921 at the age of 77.

Figure 107: Matthew Turner's obituary in the newspaper.
Source: *San Francisco Call*, February 11, 1909.

Matthew was remembered by his family as a gentleman, a passionate man, a hardworking man, a generous man, an intelligent man, a far-sighted man, a talented man, and a respected man by his family and community.[102] As Turner left the scene, it was the beginning of a change in shipbuilding. Powerful engines were replacing the sails and steel was replacing the hulls of handcrafted wood.[103]

CHAPTER ELEVEN

The Shipyard is Sold to James Robertson

James Robertson was born in San Francisco in 1873 and migrated to Scotland with his parents as an infant. At the age of 13, he returned to San Francisco in 1886 where he started to learn the shipwright's trade as an apprentice at the Union Iron Works. In 1891 he relocated to Puget Sound, Washington, where he learned wooden shipbuilding at the Hall Brothers shipyard.[104]

In 1894, Robertson returned to San Francisco and the Union Iron Works studying at night to become a naval architect. In 1903, Robertson was sent to Vladivostok, Russia, by the Union Iron Works to supervise the construction of caissons for dry docks at the Imperial Russian Naval Yard. In 1906, Robertson returned to the San Francisco shipyards and entered into a partnership with Schultz, Robertson, and Schultz. For six years Robertson designed and supervised the construction of several ferries and riverboats. When the partnership dissolved, Robertson purchased Matthew Turner's shipyard in 1913 for $20,000.[105]

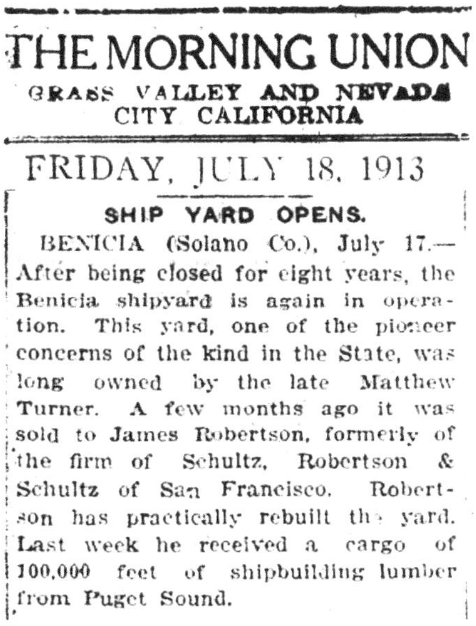

THE MORNING UNION
GRASS VALLEY AND NEVADA CITY CALIFORNIA
FRIDAY, JULY 18, 1913

SHIP YARD OPENS.

BENICIA (Solano Co.), July 17.—After being closed for eight years, the Benicia shipyard is again in operation. This yard, one of the pioneer concerns of the kind in the State, was long owned by the late Matthew Turner. A few months ago it was sold to James Robertson, formerly of the firm of Schultz, Robertson & Schultz of San Francisco. Robertson has practically rebuilt the yard. Last week he received a cargo of 100,000 feet of shipbuilding lumber from Puget Sound.

Figure 108: Announcement of the reopening of the Benicia shipyard.
Source: *The Morning Union*, July 18, 1913.

Following his purchase, the shipyard was renamed the Robertson Shipyard. Robertson added several features to facilitate shipbuilding and repair. To the west of Turner's ways, Richardson built wooden sideways with steam winches used to haul out flat-bottomed barges for repairs. Atop concrete foundations cut into the bluff of the shoreline, he built a small engine house complex to power the sideways steam wrenches. Robertson also added two end ways close to Turner's end ways and a small railway to accommodate small craft to the east of the ways.

James Robertson built several ships at the shipyard. One of the first vessels he built was a paddlewheel steam ferry called the *Charles Van Damme*. In 1914, prominent San Francisco businessman Charles Van Damme was convinced to invest in a car ferry line between Point Richmond and Marin. The Richmond-San Rafael Ferry & Transportation Company was created, and they ordered a ferry from James Robertson. The *Charles Van Damme* was completed in 1916 and placed into service carrying cars from Marin to Richmond.

Figure 109: Workers at the Richardson Shipyard stand in front of the *Charles Van Damme* ferry. Source: Museum of History Benicia.

In 1941, the U.S. Navy acquired the *Charles Van Damme* ferry to serve its large Mare Island Naval Shipyard in Vallejo. In 1944, the *Charles Van Damme* was sold off by the Navy (with the war still ongoing in the Pacific and in Europe) with the high bidder being the city of Martinez.[106] The ferry worked the Martinez-Benicia run until decommissioned in 1956. and in 1958 it was converted into a restaurant at Jack London Square. In 1959, Donlon Arques bought her at auction and brought her to her final resting place at Gate 6 in Sausalito. Here she becomes home to Juanita's Kitchen and then a fancy nightclub. Finally, the infamous "Ark" became a center for the emerging houseboat community.

In 1916, Robertson received an order from Andrew Mahoney of San Francisco to build two auxiliary four-masted schooners for the lumber trade to be named the *Rose Mahoney* and the *Andrew Mahoney*, respectively. Before they were finished, he sold them to Standard Oil Company for the selling price of $275,000 each and renamed the ships the *La Merced* and the *Oronite.*

Figure 110: *La Merced* schooner in drydock at Robertson shipyard.
Source: Museum of History Benicia.

Figure 111: *Oronite* schooner in drydock at Robertson shipyard.
Source: Museum of History Benicia.

Following the sale of the ships built for Standard Oil, Robertson built ships for

Andrew Mahoney. Named the *Rose Mahoney* and the *Andrew Mahoney*, they were five-masted schooners, 2051-ton capacity, 261 feet long, with 1800 board feet lumber capacity. The *Rose Mahoney* was launched on March 11, 1918.

Figure 112: Workers stand in front of the *Rose Mahoney* and *Andrew Mahoney* under construction in February 1917. The *Andrew Mahoney* was renamed the *Oronite*.
Source: Museum of History Benicia.

Figure 113: James Robertson's son, Russel, on the deck of the *Rose Mahoney* being built at the Robertson Shipyard in Benicia. Source: Museum of History Benicia.

As World War I approached, there was a growing interest in wooden shipbuilding. In 1916, the Robertson shipyard experienced a surge in business. Robertson eventually sold his stake in the yard to the Benicia Shipbuilding Company for $100,000 towards the end of the war. However, he stayed on as superintendent to oversee the construction of five "Ferris" design steamers, each 270 feet in length, coal-fired, with a capacity of 3,500 tons, and built for the Emergency Fleet Corporation. In 1918, Robertson left Benicia when the business moved to Alameda. While in Alameda, Robertson constructed several ferries, including the *City of Richmond* (1921), the *Aven J. Hanford* (1922), the *Golden Gate* (1923), the *Golden West* (1923), and the *City of San Rafael* (1924).[107]

In 1919, a property assessment of the Benicia shipyard structures indicated they were in good condition and valued at $3,465. After 1919, the smaller structures were torn down to avoid payment of taxes, and the shipyard was allowed to slowly deteriorate.

The shipyard was abandoned and forgotten for many years. In 1983, the area was preserved and converted into a 30-acre public park known as the "West 12th Street Park." In 1987, the site of the shipyard was designated California Historical Landmark No. 973, and is now known as the "Matthew Turner Shipyard Park."

Figure 114: Matthew Turner Shipyard Park along the Carquinez Strait at the foot of West 12th Street, Benicia.
Source: Photograph by author, 2024.

Figure 115: Matthew Turner Shipyard site at low tide, 1980s.
Source: James P. Delgado, National Park Service.

Figure 116: Matthew Turner Shipyard Park site where the capstan footing was installed.
Source: Photograph by author, 2024.

In September 1993, Matthew Turner Elementary School opened in Benicia. The Dolphin was chosen to be Turner Elementary School's mascot because they possess the qualities of speed, intelligence, and helpfulness valued by Matthew Turner himself.

Chapter Twelve
Tales of Matthew Turner's Ships

The Pacific Ocean is a rough and unpredictable sea. The ships who traversed the ocean had their share of hard knocks, grazing rocks in uncharted waters, getting dismasted by heavy seas in Pacific storms, and running aground in coastal fog. Matthew Turner's vessels, although fast and sturdy, could not always survive the forces of nature.

The Tale of the Schooner *J. C. Ford*

Figure 117: Schooner *J. C. Ford* loading lumber in Mendocino Harbor, circa 1885.
Source: Kelley House Museum.

The schooner *J. C. Ford* was built in 1882 for Jerome C. Ford, owner of the Mendocino Lumber Company, by Matthew Turner's shipyard in San Francisco. On May 14, 1882, the *J. C. Ford* entered the Mendocino port on her maiden voyage.

On December 12, 1885, three hundred miles east of Honolulu, the *J. C. Ford*, under Captain T. H. Griffiths, was struck by a falling meteor that blasted the mainmast and staysail and set everything on fire. For a few minutes, great excitement prevailed on board, but the captain and crew quickly set to work to put out the fire on the mast and sails, the latter of which was cut away and thrown overboard. Water was hauled up in buckets from the masthead and the fire was soon extinguished. Pieces of the meteor that fell on deck were red hot and resembled burning lava. The captain preserved several pieces.

Such odd fiery encounters followed the ship to its tragic end. On February 2, 1893, the schooner foundered in a squall at the entrance to Gray's Harbor, Washington, and lost the rudder. The crew had no way to steer and could only manipulate the sails. For two days they pumped water out of the hold. But when the water reached barrels of quicklime stored in the cargo area, the white powder reacted with the seawater and released enough heat to ignite the ship. Fortunately, the eight-man crew was 25 miles off the coast, within the shipping lanes, and attracted the attention of the British sailing schooner *Brenda*, who saw the distress signals and rescued the crew as the beautiful *J. C. Ford* sank from sight.[108]

The Tale of the Schooner *Emma Claudina*

Figure 118: Brigantine *Emma Claudina*, circa 1885. Source: Matson Ocean Shipping and Logistics.

Captain William Matson purchased the *Emma Claudina*, a 126-foot, 195-ton capacity brigantine from Matthew Turner in 1882. On April 23, he sailed into Hilo Bay, Hawaii, carrying 300 tons of food, plantation supplies, and general merchandise. Although he had sailed to the Hawaiian Islands before, this was his first voyage as a Captain and majority owner of his vessel.

Later that same year, in 1882, Captain Matson founded the Matson Navigation Company, which has grown to become one of the largest container ship companies in the world. In 1887, he sold the *Emma Claudina* and bought the newly built brigantine *Lurline* from Matthew Turner for $26,000. The *Lurline* had more than double the carrying capacity of his previous vessel.[109]

The Tale of the Schooner *Santa Cruz*

Figure 119: Schooner *Santa Cruz*.
Source: Islapedia, schooner *Santa Cruz*.

In 1869, Justinian Caire and a group of businessmen from San Francisco purchased Santa Cruz Island, which is located in Southern California. By the 1880s, Caire became the sole owner of the island and added a vineyard and other businesses to the existing sheep and cattle ranch. However, by 1893, the need for a dedicated shipping vessel had become apparent. As a result, a 2-masted schooner named *Santa Cruz*, with a capacity of 45 tons, was commissioned and built at the Matthew Turner Shipyard in Benicia.

Caire formed the Santa Cruz Island Company and bought the schooner *Santa Cruz* in 1893. This ship was used to transport barrels of wine from Santa Cruz to Santa Barbara for bottling and sale. However, prohibition in January 1919 put a stop to this business. Every year, the *Santa Cruz* carried many ranch hands from the mainland to the island to perform sheep roundup and shearing. On September 19, 1913, the *Santa Cruz* ran aground and Captain Nidever and the crew left the vessel, rowing towards Santa Barbara in the fog. After it was repaired, the *Santa Cruz* continued to operate as a cargo and transportation schooner for the next 23 years without facing significant issues. During World War II, it even carried soldiers back and forth to the island. The *Santa Cruz* served its homeport of Prisoner's Harbor for 67 years, making it one of the longest-operating cargo schooners on the Pacific West Coast.[110]

The Tale of the Schooner *Equator*

Figure 120: Schooner *Equator* with (left to right) Lloyd Osbourne, Robert Louis Stevenson, Fanny Van de Grift Stevenson, Mr. Rick (agent for Wightman Bros), and Captain Dennis Reid, June 30, 1889.
Source: Joe Strong photographer, c/o Writers' Museum, The Edinburgh Museums Service.

The schooner *Equator* was designed by Matthew Turner and built at his yard in Benicia for the Wightman Brothers, commission merchants, of San Francisco. Given Turner's business interests in the South Seas, the *Equator* was small at around 70 gross tons and was intended for the copra (coconut oil extract) trade between the West Coast and the islands of the South Pacific. A year after its launch, in March 1889, it sailed through and survived the South Pacific tropical cyclone that destroyed American and German warships and numerous merchantmen at Samoa.

In mid-year 1889, the *Equator* was chartered by Robert Louis Stevenson, author of *Treasure Island* and *Dr. Jekyll and Mr. Hyde*, who sailed with his wife Fanny Van de Grift Stevenson from Honolulu to the Gilbert Islands. The voyage became the basis for Stevenson's travelogue *In the South Seas*. Also present was Lloyd Osbourne, writer and Scottish stepson of Stevenson.

The *Equator* went off to other islands leaving the Stevenson party behind to enjoy two months on the beautiful Abemama atoll. They lived in four light huts that Tembinok, the High Chief of the Gilbert Islands, had ordered to be carried to a favorable spot (they called this "Equator Town"). It was here that Stevenson and Lloyd Osbourne started to write *The Wrecker* (published in 1892), inspired by a story of obscure maritime crimes that they had heard in Honolulu. The *Equator* returned on October 19 and they left on October 25, going first north to Butaritari for a short stop and then southeast for Samoa, where they arrived on December 7. Stevenson describes his stay on Abemama in Part V of *In the South Seas* (1896).[111]

In March 1897, the *Equator* was equipped with a steam engine by the Fulton Engineering and Shipbuilding Company in Oakland, California. She was then called a steamer. At the end of the month, the *Equator* was out in the bay testing her engines and collided with the tug *Alert* while docking the Howard Street wharf in San Francisco. The bowsprit of the *Equator* was torn away and her head was lost before she backed away.[112] Captain Lazzervich was immediately discharged by the owners, Hume Brothers & Hume.

In February 1899, the *Equator* had 15 feet of length added to her stern. She was used in delivering salmon from the Alaska canneries to San Fransisco.[113]

In 1915, the *Equator* arrived in Seattle when it was purchased by the Cary-Davis Tug and Barge Company for use as a tugboat. In 1916, it was chartered by the U.S. Coast and Geodetic Survey to conduct coastal surveying in Alaska. *Equator* spent her final years as a tugboat until 1956 when she was abandoned on the coast of Jetty Island outside Everett as part of a breakwater with other discarded vessels. It remained there for 11 years as part of a breakwater.

Across the subsequent decades, various plans to preserve and house the *Equator* were proposed and fell through and the funds necessary for a full restoration were never acquired. Reduced to a hulk, the vessel was moved in 1980 to the Port of Everett's Marina Village and later to the corner of 10th Street and Craftsman Way.

The Port of Everett has other plans to honor the *Equator's* legacy. Some of the ship's timbers are slated to be used in public art installations along the waterfront. The Port is also planning to build an interpretive exhibit with a model of the *Equator* at the Waterfront Center and a ship-themed playground at Jetty Landing near the 10th Street boat launch.

The Tale of the Schooner *Dora*

Figure 121: The half-brigantine steamship *Dora*, circa 1900.
Source: Museum of History Benicia.

Captain Matthew Turner, oversaw the construction of the steamship *Dora* for the Alaska Commercial Company and specifically for its future president, the seal hunter Louis Schloss in 1879. The *Dora*, constructed of Puget Sound pine, measured 27 feet across, and her gross capacity weight was 320 tons. Her draft was 13.2 feet and she was powered by an 80-horsepower "compound single-screw engine," and a two-bladed prop measuring seven and a half feet in diameter. She was also equipped with two masts and a full set of sails.

Dora made her maiden voyage on a calm, sunny April day in 1880, from the shipyard in San Francisco to the Golden Gate Strait and back. Experienced steamship men on board wagered on her average speed and most chose between 6.75 and 7.75 knots. The fastest speed selected was 8.13 knots, but the *Dora* exceeded all expectations, recording a speed of 8.25 knots.

Owner Louis Schloss first put the *Dora* to work carrying fur seal skins from the Pribilof Islands to California for the Alaska Commercial Company. Seals in the Bering Sea were being killed by the thousands and the *Dora's* manifest was indicative of the death toll: more than 12,000 skins in 1880, and more than 15,000 in both 1881 and 1882. Soon, however, the *Dora* became most widely known as a passenger ship. And the stories about her began.

There was the rescue: hundreds of passengers and crew members saved from greater privations or certain death. There were narrow escapes including surviving the ashfall from the Mt. Katmai-Novarupta eruption in 1912. And there were the accidents, a long list of bangs and bumps, of patchwork and major repairs, of wondering which misfortune might be her last.

The ordeal for the crew of the *Dora* began ordinarily enough: Known for having the longest and most northerly mail route in the world, the steamship launched from Seward on December 2, 1905, bound for Cold Bay, Dutch Harbor, and other points westward. Despite heavy seas and some delays, she made her scheduled stops all the way west, but on the return trip, she departed Kodiak harbor on December 24 and was not seen again for two months. Typically, the *Dora's* winter mail run lasted about 20 days. This one, which was never completed, lasted four times as long.

Newspaper reports of the time state that the *Dora* was caught in rough waters approximately 15 miles away from Chignik port when the weather abruptly turned for the worse. Gale-force winds battered the 112-foot steamer, causing waves to crash over the deck. The ship's nine-foot-long boiler, made of half-inch iron and powered by a furnace capable of burning nearly 3,000 pounds of coal per day, was jolted severely, causing it to shift eight inches out of position. Steam pipes were bent and burst, cutting off the primary source of energy for the ship's engine. The crew raised the sails, but the freezing temperatures caused ice to quickly accumulate on the upper hull, rigging, and sails. The *Dora* was powerless and drifted for three weeks, with no means of radio communication and winds constantly pushing the ship farther south and out to sea. The crew could only hope to ride out the storm and wait for a warming trend.

Whenever temperatures climbed sufficiently and winter storms abated enough to use the sails, Captain Zeb Moore directed the ship toward the West Coast, once nearing Vancouver Island before being blown back out to sea. Thus, the *Dora* zigged and zagged across open water for another month. By mid-February, the *Dora* had been reported as missing. The ship, her crew, and a handful of passengers were presumed lost. Lloyd's of London prepared to issue an insurance payoff to her owners, the Northwest Steamship Company. Then, on February 24, the owners received a cablegram from Port Angeles, Washington, informing them that the *Dora* had survived, battered but intact, with all on board safe, the voyage that left the ship virtually adrift for 63 days. The *Dora* had been sighted, moving "under shredded sails," near the Strait of Juan de Fuca and had been towed to Port Angeles for repairs.

Life was tough for the ship named *Dora*. During her early years, she was used to carry passengers and freight. People living along her route joked that she managed to hit every rock and reef between Seattle and Seward, but somehow she always kept going. Later, when she was used as a mail boat, she continued to hit rocks and get stuck on sandbars. But after some quick patching to the hull or a long layover for repairs in dry-dock, she was always back in action. It seemed like the *Dora* had nine lives and always managed to survive to sail another day. On June 6, 1912, the passengers and crew of the Dora provided one of the earliest firsthand accounts of the eruption of the Mt. Katmai-Novarupta volcano.

The *Dora* traveled from the West Coast to Southeast Alaska, to Prince William Sound and Cook Inlet, to Bristol Bay and the Aleutian Islands, and occasionally to Nome. The *Dora's* 40-year career ended on December 20, 1920, when it ran aground and sank on Noble Island in British Columbia, Canada, while traveling from Seattle to Unga, a Territory of Alaska, with a cargo of general merchandise and a crew of 29 aboard. The steamship Admiral Rodman rescued 10 members of the *Dora's* crew and provided the word of the wreck.[114]

The Tale of the Brigantine *William G. Irwin*

Figure 122: Brigantine *William G. Irwin* off Diamond Head, Hawaii, 1890. Source: Jacques Denny, oil on canvas.

William G. Irwin, a brigantine of 348 tons, was built at the Matthew Turner shipyard in San Francisco in 1881 for J. D. Spreckels as a Hawaii packet. She later was transferred to the Oceanic Steamship Company, which was largely owned by the Spreckels family.

William G. Irwin was born in England in 1843 and sailed with his family for California with a cargo of merchandise immediately after the discovery of gold in 1849. The family then sailed to Hawaii. In 1880, Irwin and Claus Spreckels formed the firm W. G. Irwin & Company and for many years it was the leading sugar agency in the Hawaii Kingdom and the one originally used by the West Maui Sugar Association.

The brigantine appears several times in the list of fast passages, her best being from San Francisco to Kahului in 8 days and 17 hours in 1881. In 1886, she was sold to the Tacoma & Roche Harbor Line Company and then in 1917 was sold to Captain Alex Woodside for $28,000 for the offshore copra trade. She was rerigged a three-masted schooner of 400-ton capacity and was taken over a year later by the Bank of Italy. She was laid up in San Francisco in July 1920, after she arrived from Samoa. Two years later, she was reported going to pieces rapidly and was shortly thereafter sold to Famous Players-Lasky, an American motion picture company. She was towed to Southern California and burned for a movie at Catalina Island, on May 15, 1926.[115]

The Tale of the Schooner *Pitcairn*

Figure 123: *Pitcairn* on postage stamp
Source: Piicairn Island stamp issue 1975.

The *Pitcairn* was a schooner built in 1890 for the Seventh-day Adventist Church for use in missionary work on the Pitcairn Islands in the South Pacific. The Seventh-day Adventist representative John Tay, a former sailor, signed a detailed contract with Turner to deliver a schooner complete in "hull, spars, and iron work" on July 31, 1890, for $7,400, to be paid in installments as the work progressed. No work was to be done on Saturdays in accordance with the views of the Seventh-day Adventists. Turner agreed to donate $500 of his own money, so the cost was lowered to $6,900. The cost of the schooner when fully rigged was under $12,000, although the final cost of the fully furnished vessel was $18,683.05.

The ship had eight berths for a crew of up to twelve seamen. In addition to this, there was a galley, an 11 by 24 feet cabin with a bookcase and an organ, as well as other furniture. The ship also had six staterooms for up to eighteen passengers, along with two toilet rooms and one bathroom.

The ship was launched into San Francisco Bay on schedule on July 28, 1890, and work started on rigging and outfitting. The ship was dedicated on the afternoon of September 25, 1890, in a lengthy ceremony attended by about 1,500 people. Several short trips were made in the bay before the start of the first voyage, carrying Sabbath School members as passengers. The white-hulled *Pitcairn* was described as a fine specimen of American shipbuilding and a shapely wooden craft. At the *Pitcairn's* dedication M. C. Wilcox said the ship was "made of the very best timber" with workmanship of "the best character." One of her later captains said, "She was a smart vessel and could sail like the devil."

Pitcairn made six voyages in the South Pacific in the 1890s, carrying missionaries to the Society Islands, Cook Islands, Samoa, Tonga, and Fiji. On each of *Pitcairn's* voyages, the vessel sailed from San Francisco to Pitcairn Island before going on to other islands. Some of the islanders became interested in missionary work and asked to accompany missionaries assigned to other islands. Some of the islanders were brought to San Francisco for formal training at Healdsburg College in Northern California.

After six missionary voyages, the schooner was sold in 1900 for commercial use and renamed *Florence S*. She was lost after being stranded on the island of Mindoro, Philippine Islands, on October 17, 1912.[116]

The Tale of the Barkentine *Benicia*

Figure 124:
The Barkentine *Benicia*, circa 1900.
Source: Museum of History Benicia.

The three-masted barkentine *Benicia* was launched by Turner in September 1899 and named after the city of his shipyard. While the *Benicia* was known for a fast passage from Newcastle, New South Wales to Kehei, Hawaii, 35 days, she was a ship with a troubled history.

The *Aberdeen Herald* reported on November 30, 1899, that the newly-christened barkentine *Benicia* was making her first port call in Aberdeen, Washington, to load lumber bound for Australia.

> As it was setting to sail, a kerfuffle occurred between union and non-union sailors. The ship was manned by a non-union crew, that is they did not belong to the union, but were receiving the union scale of wages. The non-union crew on the *Benicia* reported that the union sailors in port appeared to have a hard feeling toward them and on a Friday night one of the crew of the *Benicia* was waylaid on his way to the vessel by two men, whom he said were union men, and was severely beaten.
>
> In view of this trouble, and being ready to sail on the early morning tide, Captain Bowes of the *Benicia* feared that drastic measures might be resorted to that night to prevent him from sailing with his non-union crew, and requested Marshal Graham to give him a deputy marshal to guard the ship that night. The marshal deputized Chas. Y. Fenwick who went on board in the evening. Everything passed off quietly until shortly after midnight when the captain called Fenwick down into the cabin to have a lunch that had been prepared for him by the steward. After eating lunch Fenwick and the captain, heard a noise on deck and ran for the companionway, Fenwick leading the way. As Fenwick started up the steps he was dazed by the flash and report of a discharging pistol almost in his face and heard the command to go back. Feeling a sharp sting in the eye as the pistol was discharged, a piece of lead was from the bullet as it hit an iron rod near him. Fenwick took a pistol and fired a shot up the companionway and both men rushed up onto the deck, where two shots were fired at them, passing over their heads.
>
> Reaching the deck, they found it swarming with men, as well as the wharf, The marauders had rushed into the forecastle and forced the crew out at the point of pistols, and there they were on deck partially clothed and with what few of their effects they

could grab as they ran. The captain shouted to the crew to go back below, that he would settle with the mob, which he did. Then the mob began to scatter from the ship and commenced shooting from the dock. Fenwick and the captain secured the shotgun and returned the fire, using the gun alternately. One man was seen to fall as if shot, and his comrades picked him up and scattered. The skirmish was over and dubbed the "Battle of the Wishkah." The *Benicia* sailed Sunday morning with the original crew.[117]

In September 1907, the *Santa Cruz Sentinel* reported that an argument on board the barkentine *Benicia* terminated in the arrest of Captain S. Treanor on the charge of battery at the instance of his Japanese cook, Uyehara. The difficulty arose between the captain and his employee on account of an alleged act of insubordination on Uyehara's part, and a fight ensued. Uyehara was put in irons by the captain's orders, but Uyehara escaped and, with one of the fetters dangling from his wrist, went to the office of Justice L. F. Wells and swore to a warrant charging his employer with battery.

In December 1912, the *Benicia* was lying peacefully at the docks of the Lindstrom Shipbuilding Company in Aberdeen waiting for an overhauling after returning from Mexico. There was no indication of the tragedy that was enacted on her decks before the vessel left the Mexican port, in which the cook, Teddy Weise, killed First Mate Anderson, and then committed suicide. Weise, according to the story, also attempted to kill the second mate, Harry Uddy, and would have carried out his plan but for Uddy's quick work in throwing a lamp at the madman's head and escaping the shot that was intended for him. The lamp exploded killing Weise. The bodies of Weise and Anderson were buried by the local authorities.[118]

The *Benicia* was owned by Nelson Andrews and was sold to J. J. Moore & Company in 1917. She was again sold to H. G. Seaborn of Seattle, Washington. The *Benicia* continued to run in the lumber trade to Hawaii and Tahiti for years. The vessel was finally owned by Whitney and Bodden of New Orleans. The *Benicia* met its end when it was wrecked on Lafolle Reef off Haiti on October 10, 1920.

The Tale of the Schooner *Tolna*

Figure 125: Schooner *Tolna* (right).
Source: *Tribal Arts, In Search of Adventure,* March 2020.

The *Tolna*, a schooner yacht of 82 tons was built in 1893 at the Turner shipyard for Count Festetics von Tolna. Count Rudolf Festetics was born in Paris on September 17, 1865, to Hungarian parents. He studied at the Theresianum, a school for noble youths. Following his studies, he served some years in Hungary as a Hussar lieutenant. After his discharge from the cavalry, he took several short trips through Europe and Africa and later traveled to the United States. The educated young count became a favorite of the local financial elite in short order. In 1892, he married Ella Haggen, the only daughter of a prominent Washington millionaire. He spent her dowry on the construction of the schooner *Tolna* at Matthew Turner's shipyard in Benicia.[119] "I saw every piece of wood that went into her. She was luxuriously furnished, commodious, and a fine sailer," said Turner.[120] The count and his wife sailed to the South Seas on their seven-year honeymoon in October 1893. Before they had reached Hawaii the crew of their ship, former pirates, attempted to take the couple hostage and imprison them on an uninhabited island for ransom. Festetics managed to prevent this and delivered them, cowed, and beaten to the authorities in Hawaii. During the remainder of the voyage mutinies, tempests, and other difficulties were interspersed with romantic but dangerous expeditions to the various Pacific islands they visited.

In 1899, shortly before the end of his first voyage, Festetics' wife left him in Singapore. Several years later, the *Tolna* became stranded on Minicoy Island, north of the Maldives, and the Count had no choice but to empty the ship of his priceless ethnographic collection, and burned the boat that had carried him so far. After what must have seemed like an interminable wait for rescue, but finally he succeeded in finding his way home on a merchant ship. He landed in Trieste to discover that Ella had divorced him. Festetics finally returned to Vienna where he wrote two volumes about his voyages, which were published in French.

The Tale of the Schooner *Mascotte*

The *Los Angeles Herald* published the article titled *Cannibal Islanders of the South Seas*[121] on November 15, 1900.

> With a cannibal crew and stories of narrow escapes from the man-eaters of New Britain and New Ireland, the gasoline schooner *Mascotte* came into the port of San Francisco late Tuesday night November 14. The *Mascotte* was built in Benicia by Matthew Turner, two years ago, for Hernsheim & Co. of Hamburg. Hernsheim has over thirty trading stations in the Southern seas, fully half of them located on islands where the natives are all cannibals. On several occasions, Captain Macco of the *Mascotte* and his men had narrow escapes, while the vessel bears the marks of the troubles she was in. Foresail and mainsail are riddled with bullets, the rail forward is splintered from contact with Mauser bullets, two bullet holes are in the deck and the engineer's room is perforated.
>
> "On August 29," Captain Macco said "We were heading for Komuli, one of our stations in the Admiralty group. As we made port, I was surprised to see three canoes laden with men making off to the southward. I was still more surprised to find that when we came within range a hail of bullets began to pour down on us. The natives had procured guns from somewhere and were firing at us from the brush. We have a little four-pounder (cannon) aboard, and when I got that to work the natives soon scattered.
>
> "As soon as the firing ceased, I got a boat and went ashore. It did not take long to show me that the station had been looted,

and H. Matzeke, the agent, and ten of his boys, brought from the Carolines, had been killed and eaten. The pots were still on the fire, and simmering in them were various portions of the human body. The devils had evidently been preparing for a wind-up feast when we surprised them. The guns with which they fired at us were stolen from the trader's house.

"While we lay at anchor that day three native boys swam out to us. They had belonged to Matzeke's gang and had escaped by a miracle. All of them had been cut and wounded in the melee, but they got into the bush and hid there till we came along. One of the boys told the story of the massacre as follows: Some of the men were down at the beach and some were asleep. Chief Rew and one of his men came along and wanted to trade some native money for some cloth.

"In order to understand what follows," Captain Macco said "You must remember that in the New Hebrides, the New Solomon group, and New Guinea all the money is a species of shell, strung on cocoanut fiber. As much as a man can stretch with his arms extended is worth so much in trade. Now, when Chief Rew wanted to trade with Matzeke, he offered him a string of native money. As soon as Matzeke spread out his arms to measure the stuff, the native who accompanied the chief struck him on the back of the neck and knocked him senseless. He was dispatched in a few minutes by the warriors who lay in waiting. Then the massacre began.

"When I found out how my countryman had been killed and eaten, I went ashore with my gun and all my men, and we drove the natives to the hills and set fire to the village. Then I went back to Kasi and reported to the captain of the German sloop-of-war the *Seeadler*. He at once got up steam we went together back to Komuli. The natives fled into the interior, but we destroyed eighty villages, killed about one hundred and sixty inhabitants and took twenty prisoners. The prisoners are now working on a breakwater in German New Guinea.

"At Matty Island, in the Solomons, we met a warm reception. We sent a supercargo and two traders ashore and only landed a firing party in time to save them from the pot. We encountered a shower of spears, but when I opened on them with my Winchester they were scared to death. A firearm had never been heard on Matty Island before, and when their men began to drop one by one, and after each report they saw a man with a gaping wound in his body and blood flowing, they got scared and fled to the hills in a hurry. We established a trading station there, but someday the trader may meet the same fate as Mr. Matzeke.

"My crew of eighteen are nearly all from the islands of New Britain and New Ireland, while a few are from New Guinea. Every one of them has dined on human flesh, but they are terribly afraid of a gun. We carry an arsenal of twelve Mauser rifles, six Krag-Jorgensons, twelve Winchesters, and six revolvers. Every gun is loaded and ready for use.

"The engineer had a narrow escape one day. He was firing at the natives, who were throwing spears and shooting arrows when he ran short of ammunition. Just as he stepped out of his room a shot crashed through the roof and went through the chair where he had been sitting. "

All's well that ends fairly well, however, and we'll give the cannibals another rub next spring."

In July 1901, on the *Mascotte* return trip to the South Seas, the vessel caught fire and burned in Konig Albert Strait (between Buka and Bougainville).

The Tale of the Pilot Schooner *America*

Figure 126: Pilot Schooner *America* in San Francisco with Fort Point in the background.
Source: The Hunt Family.

The *America*, a pilot schooner of 74 tons and 81 feet long, was built at the Matthew Turner shipyard in Benicia in July 1888 for the association called the 20 Bar Pilots of San Francisco. The contract price was $15,000 and she would be the largest boat ever built for the pilot service on the West Coast. The delivery of the *America* was delayed by the bar pilots until the first of October, an she remained in Benicia.

The *Alta Californian* reported, "On her trial down from Benicia she proved herself a remarkable sailer. The suit of sails is a beautiful fit and reflects great credit to the makers, Fraser & Holihan of 11 Drumm Street. They set as flat as a board without a wrinkle, and add much beauty to the craft."

On September 15, a regatta was held using the "old" San Francisco course; a line from Mission Rock to Cattle Wharf, to Hunters Point, then to the stake boat off Fort Point, and back over the same course to the starting line. The race featured the new schooner *Charles H. White*, and the new pilot boat *America*, which was sailed by Captain Turner, and four other ships. Owing to the lack of wind, the race started at 1 P. M.

The race started and the *Charles H. White* caught a light offshore breeze and took a good lead. Halfway to Hunters Point, the breeze was calm, allowing the *America* to pull ahead of the *Charles H. White,* and the other yachts were also catching up. The breeze strengthened and spectators saw one of the prettiest sights on the bay: six yachts close together, almost abreast, heading for Oakland. The breeze strengthened and the *America* had a commanding lead, The *Charles H. White*, seeing herself irretrievably in the rear, tacked into Meiggs Wharf at San Francisco, giving up the race.

Charlie White was not satisfied that the *America* was the faster craft and would wager a thousand dollars on this craft. The challenge was accepted by the owners of the *America* and a race around the Farallon Islands was proposed. Ten days were given for the vessels to prepare for the race. The ships were metalized in which the hulls of the ships were covered in copper sheets.

The big race was set for Saturday, September 29, 1888, as the *America* would go into commission as a pilot boat on October 1. The challenge, known as the *Aggie-Lurline* course, was around the Farallon Islands and back. Captain Turner would command the wheel of the *America* and Captain Sam Stanton would master the *C. H. White.*

At 8 o'clock in the morning, the boats were towed out by the tugboat *Sea Lion* from Pilot's Cove to the starting point. The ships cast off at 10 am, and the *America* showed to its advantage a set of new Fraser & Holihan sails which filled like boards and pulled like racehorses. The sea was perfectly still and the wind was light when the *C. H. White* crossed the start line at 10:04:50; the *America* crossed at 10:09:26. The *C. H. White* headed directly into the sea and took advantage of a strong on-shore breeze. She had a lead a half of a mile windward, and a half a mile ahead. The *America* headed toward the northern coast, then caught a good full breeze and began to cut down the lead.

By this time, the ships were in blue water, the sun had melted the cloudbanks and the Farallons were in plain view. Bit by bit the *America* clewed into the wind until she was able to point directly at her goal.

Nearing the Farallons, Captain Stanton was split between sailing close around the rocks sacrificing speed, or going full-tacking windward for speed. His efforts resulted in a 12-minute rounding of the Farallons. The *America* had a commanding position and made a beautiful turn windward around the rock, losing no distance, in 2 minutes. Once squared away, her sails fluttered into position and she was driving home at an incredible speed. As the breeze freshened, she increased her lead to six miles and sailed joyfully into the bay as the winner. The race, 59 miles, was won with a time of 6 hours and 45 ½ minutes, an event that was never repeated with such vessels on the San Francisco Bay.

Although Matthew didn't intend to humiliate Charlie White, he ended up doing so. Matthew had created a unique design, which he called the Pacific design. He wasn't challenging Charlie White as a person, but rather his principles.[122]

Tale of the Schooner *Courtney Ford*

Figure 127: Schooner *Courtney Ford* with her deck full of lumber, c1892.
Source: Jenny Bartlet, *Sailing Rigs*, US Naval Institute Press.

Figure 128: *Courtney Ford* billet head carving.
Source: Robert Shaw, Alaska State Historic Preservation Officer.

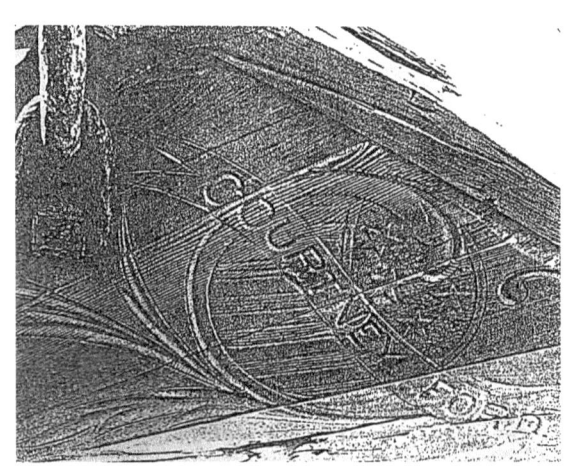

The schooner *Courtney Ford* was built by Turner at his shipyard in Benicia in 1883. The two-masted, 401-ton vessel, was 146 feet long, and a spacious 34 feet in the beam. This translates into a cargo capacity of a half million board feet of lumber or 300 gross tons of break-bulk goods like sugar, wheat, and fruit, all common trade goods of the day. Sailed by a crew of eight to ten, the *Courtney Ford* was loaded with lumber within days of launching.

Courtney Ford's career began by hauling fruit from Suva and Fiji to San Francisco, dry goods and materials to Tahiti, and sugar cane from Honolulu, Hawaii. She chartered out on her mainstay coastwise trade: hauling lumber on numerous voyages from the Puget Sound sawmill towns to growing towns and cities all along the Pacific seaboard from Alaska to California.

On September 7, 1902, the *Courtney Ford* was northbound out of Everett in Puget Sound for Unga Island with gold mining supplies and equipment for the Apollo Mine when she was caught in a typhoon in the Gulf of Alaska. Captain N. E. Burgeson and his crew were well seasoned, sailing in good weather and bad. But this autumn voyage found them lost in the pernicious fog common to the Aleutian Islands in summer and fall. Thinking the lookout had spotted Akun Island, with the fairway through Unimak Pass off the port bow, Captain Burgeson ordered the sails let out for a bit more speed. They heard the roar of breakers before sighting a faint white line of foaming waves through the fog dead ahead. Startled, Burgeson ordered the men to turn her away from the wind. But before the crew even reached the rigging she was slammed by a williwaw (the descent of cold, dense air from coastal mountains) went hard aground past the breakers, and stranded herself high on the beach. The impact flung two men off the deck to their immediate deaths in the pounding waves. Burgeson was dumbfounded as there was no way a sandy beach was on their plotted course.

Suspecting the compass, he tore apart the housing that sits in front of the ship's wheel. To his disgust and rage, he discovered small pieces of iron had been inserted into the space around the compass, causing it to give grossly inaccurate readings. He laid it to 'the dastardly work of some miscreant' who had it in for the ship or the crew while at St. Michael. Fearing the ship might break up as morning dawned gray and raining, he ordered the crew to set up camp where they remained for a week hoping to spot a passing ship for assistance.

By now they reckoned the beach was the long spit-like Glen Island fronting Izembek Lagoon on the Alaska Peninsula. The Aleut village of Morzhovoi was somewhere nearby and traffic out of the busy post-salmon season of Bristol Bay might come close enough to Amak Island in the distance to see their signals. The mate and several men rowed the ship's skiff to search for the village. The second of the tragic loss of lives happened when the skiff capsized in the surf, drowning two more sailors.

They got lucky when a passing vessel spied their signal fire. Burgeson assigned Seaman William Ode to remain with the *Courtney Ford* while he and the remaining crew went for help. On October 23, 1902, Burgeson and his four remaining crewmen arrived aboard the schooner *Centennial* at the Seattle docks. Nothing was heard of Seaman Ode until eight months later. Captain Lundquist of the steamer *St. Paul* southbound out of Nome, which arrived in Seattle in late June, had obtained the log William Ode kept. His last entry was February 19, 1903 "One month since I laid up with the schooner. Life is sweet, but death is sweeter in a case like this. I have nothing but cold scraps and snow water. Today I ate some dried apples and a piece of ice. I can make no more fire, as I can't stay up that long." The last entry is faint, the letters shaky: "Death at last. Four months alone."[123]

In 1980, the site and remains of the *Courtney Ford* schooner's hull at Glenn Island, Alaska, were listed on the National Register of Historic Places.

The Tale of the Brigantine *Tahiti*

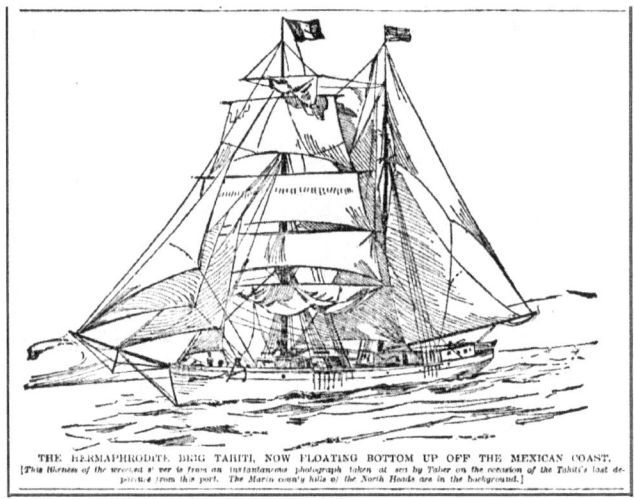

Figure 129: Newspaper sketch of the brigantine *Tahiti*.
Source: *San Francisco Examiner*, November 30, 1891.

The *Tahiti* was built in San Francisco in 1881 by Matthew Turner. She was 290 tons burden and one of the fastest sailers in the San Francisco to Tahiti packet line trade for ten years. She was sold in December 1890 to H. H. Leavitt of New York and Captain W. H. Ferguson, as the newly built brigantine *Galilee* was ready to take over her packet line.[124]

A dispatch from Manzanillo, Mexico, on November 29, 1891, stated that the steamer *Roseville* arrived and reported passing at sea the wreck of the brig *Tahiti*. The *Tahiti* was said to be used as a slaver ship loaded with 270 natives from the South Sea islands, who were to work on sugar and coffee plantations.[125]

The *San Francisco Call* reported the *Tahiti* left here on April 5, 1891, for Butaritari, an atoll in the Pacific Ocean island nation of Kiribati, via Honolulu, with miscellaneous cargo for trading purposes. After the cargo was disposed of, 270 natives of the Gilbert Islands were taken aboard after attractive inducements were offered, and they were bound to labor on Mexican plantations in San Benito, Mexico, for three years at $8 a month. They had virtually sold themselves into slavery for three years.

During the 19th and 20th centuries, a practice known as "blackbirding" took place on a large scale with the taking of indigenous people from numerous islands in the South Pacific. It was the coercion of people through deception or kidnapping to work as slaves or poorly paid laborers in countries distant from their native land.

On the trip to Mexico in August, the *Tahiti* was driven northward by a storm, and put in at Drakes Bay, California, on September 4 for repairs of the hull and rigging. After the repairs, Captain Ferguson and surgeon Dr. Gibson left the vessel and were succeeded by Captain C. Erickson and physician Dr. Harry Serymser. The crew was replaced by a Scandinavian crew.[126]

Reports in reference to the cargo of Gilbert Island natives reached the ears of the US Treasury Agents, but the Government could not interfere because the ship's manifest showed that the natives were merely passengers on the vessel and not held against their will.

Dr. Gibson who was the surgeon on the ship from Butaritari to Drakes Bay had the following comments.

> "The islanders taken on board the *Tahiti* were a mix of men, women, and children. All had a good opinion of Mexico and were anxious to go. Those who shipped were given clothing – the men's shirts, blouses, and overalls, and the women's calico shirts of the mother-Hubbard pattern. They had plenty of bunks and were given as much food as they wanted with as much fresh stuff as could be had or went to the crew. They were never abused, and there was no slave business about it. They were not over-intelligent, but they knew exactly where they were going, and they wanted to go. They were never treated badly during the whole forty days from the islands to Point Reyes. In fact, it

was more like a missionary ship than anything else, and there were religious ceremonies every morning." [127]

The brig sailed from Drakes Bay on September 8 and should have reached her destination later that month. None of the *Tahiti's* passengers have been heard from since she sailed southward from Drakes Bay. it was feared that all on board perished as well as the Captain, the physician, three mates, and the crew of two cooks and twelve seamen. It was believed the ship encountered a "chubasco," a violent squall with thunder and lightning, occurring during the rainy season along the Pacific coast of Mexico.

An attempt was made to find the *Tahiti* as there was a perception that she had a considerable amount of money on board, as there were several wealthy men on board who were interested in the business she was engaged in.

She was found by Captain Smith of the California Cod Fishing Company. Captain Smith left Manzanillo on November 25 on the steamer *Roseville*, having in tow the schooner *Vine*. On the following day, they sighted the wreck of the *Tahiti* eleven miles southwest of Lizard Point, the islands are off Mazatlán on the coast of Mexico. The ill-fated vessel was reported to have been seen floating bottom up with the rudder gone, and the name *Tahiti of San Francisco* being distinctly visible on the stern.

In an attempt to tow the *Tahiti* back to shore, the steamer let go of the schooner *Vine*, and it hooked up a tow line to the wreck. They towed for twenty-four hours but made but little progress, the tow line parted several times. Each time it parted the Mexican crew had to dive down and attach again to one of the bow anchors which hung down eleven fathoms. At this time the wreck was eighty-five miles from Manzanillo and finding it impossible to make any headway, the *Roseville* steamed back to procure a more powerful steamer to tow the wreck. The amount of $100 a day was offered for the steamer *Mazatlán* to do the job. The hull of the *Tahiti* was worth $5,000, independent of what may be found in the cabin and in the hold. It was expected that steamers would go after the wreck on the last of November or the 1st of December, and they expected to take a valuable prize.

Further attempts to tow the Tahiti to shore failed. But in April 1892, the US cruiser *Boston* stationed in San Diego received orders from the Navy Department at Washington to search the Revilla Giodo islands for the shipwrecked sailors and islanders supposed to have been lost. All the islands were thoroughly searched without finding any castaways or any traces of the vessel.[128]

In July, a story in the *Los Angeles Herald* reported that Leon Martell of San Diego said two of those supposed to have been drowned by the capsizing of the brig *Tahiti* escaped death and were seen by Martell in April, about sixty miles from Manzanilla, Mexico. Later he was told by Felix Johansen, a 33-year-old Finnish crew member survivor, that when the brig capsized he and four Gilbert islanders, including a woman, alone succeeded in leaving the vessel. They were stranded for sixteen days in an open boat without food or water. The woman died on the fourth day and the men ate portions of her flesh to keep themselves alive. One of the islanders became insane from drinking salt water and jumped overboard and the third man died from exposure. Johansen and the fourth islander finally succeeded in making shore and were cared for by fishermen.[129]

Matthew Turner was astounded when he read about the incident.

> *She was one of the best vessels built on this coast. She was a rapid sailer and as staunch and steady as a church. I can't conceive how she could have capsized unless she was insufficiency ballasted. My explanation is that very little ballast was placed in the brig, and the captain depended on full water casks for ballast. Such a crowd as was on board would consume a great deal of water, and if the casks were not filled with salt water as they were emptied of fresh water, the brig must have been very light. All the people were above the water line, and if a squall struck the ship they would be blown to the leeward side, and their weight would have some effect in turning the vessel.*[130]

Tale of the Yacht *Chispa*

Figure 130: The yacht *Chispa*
Source: Museum of History Benicia

The yacht *Chispa* was built in 1879 by Matthew Turner in his San Francisco shipyard. The yacht was sold to Matthew's friend Commodore Isadore Gutte who was affiliated with the San Francisco Yacht Club. The *Chispa* participated in San Francisco Yacht Club races and was known to be one of the fastest yachts in San Francisco Bay. She was a common sight in the 1880s and 1890s.

In August 1898 Captain James Morse Brooks, navigator of the yacht *Chispa*, signed a contract with Captain Turner of Benicia for the construction of a two-story scow to cost $1,400. The dimensions would be 100 feet in length with a 45-foot beam, and the upper deck would have a number of staterooms. The scow would be known as a marine restaurant, and every kind of fish would be served. The scow will be anchored in Horseshoe Bay located near the Golden Gate.[131]

On September 24, 1898, the Chispa was anchored about 200 yards off the San Francisco Yacht Clubhouse. A group of men onshore heard gunshots and a few concerned citizens and lawmen got into small boats to investigate. They discovered that Captain James Morse Brooks had been murdered while asleep in his bunk on the vessel. Peter Nelson, a deckhand, claimed that the crime was committed by "two men, one tall and the other short," and that he escaped death by jumping overboard and swimming for his life. The circumstances were so unusual that the authorities believed it was justified to arrest Nelson as a suspect and confined him in a cell in the San Rafael Jail. Investigators found that robbery had been the motive as they found the pockets of all the clothing in the room were turned inside out, the drawers of the lockers drawn forth, and the room in a topsy-turvy condition. On the floor was found a common ice pick covered with blood.

Nelson's vivid description of the tall man on deck was precise and detailed. However, when questioned about how he could discern so much in the dim light and why he had hurriedly jumped overboard, he started to falter and became unclear about some details. The deckhand was rescued within two minutes after jumping overboard, yet none of the onlookers from the shore saw a boat leaving the yacht. Subsequently, Nelson was arrested, and several news outlets covered his detention and the ongoing investigation. However, I found no reports of a trial, leaving the mystery unresolved. Notably, Captain Brooks' planned two-story scow restaurant was never constructed.

On November 14, 1898, the *Sacramento Daily Union* reported a story *"The Chispa Again,"* this time a watchman was shot on the yacht. They reported Nick Berg was shot and fatally wounded about 9 o'clock on the yacht *Chispa* at Sausalito by Ike Elk. Both men were employed as watchmen, It appears that Bergs's infatuation for Elk's wife was the immediate cause of the shooting, as the men were known to have frequently quarreled over the woman.

Berg rowed over to the *Chispa* where Elk and his wife were on board. Elk stepped aboard and immediately opened fire, then jumped into a boat and made his way to shore. He was stopped by police and told the officers that he had shot a man whom he thought was a burglar. Elk was placed under arrest and after he had told his story, he declined to talk further about the case. On November 28, Nick Burge was released from the county jail as no charge had been placed against him.

The *Chispa* returned to racing without any other incidents. On February 26, 1908, Isadore Gutte passed away at age 76. The *Chispa* was sold by the Gutte estate to the California Yacht Club.[132] The *Chispa* was captained by Charles Chittenden from 1915 to 1918. On October 16, 1936, the San Francisco Yacht Club took the *Chispa* to the San Rafael Creek basin where the pleasure craft has remained.[133]

Tale of the Brigantine *Karluk*

Figure 131: The half-brigantine steamer *Karluk* in ice, September 1913.
Source: Newfoundland and Labrador Heritage.

The half-brigantine steamer *Karluk* was built in 1884 by Matthew Turner at his Benicia shipyard for the Karluk Packing Company. The company used the vessel for its sockeye salmon fishing and canning business on the Karluk River, a stream 24 miles long, on Kodiak Island in Alaska.

In 1889 the Alaska Improvement Company began canning at the Karluk River, across from the Karluk Spit. The river's enormous runs of sockeye salmon easily supplied the entire cannery demand of 58,000 fish in 1882 Harvests continued to increase each year and reached 1,004,800 in 1887.[134] In 1911 the canning operations were transferred to Larsen Bay located 16 miles away.

The brigantine *Karluk* was repurposed for whaling in 1908 as it was no longer required for its original purpose. To make the vessel sturdier, its bows and sides were covered with 2-inch Australian ironwood. Despite having gone on 14 arctic whaling voyages, including six winter expeditions, the ship was not designed to endure continuous ice pressure and lacked the engine power to push through the ice.

In 1913, Vilhjalmur Stefansson, a Canadian anthropologist, purchased the *Karluk* for $10,000. The purpose of the purchase was to use the ship as part of the Canadian Arctic Expedition, which was a scientific expedition that took place in the Arctic Circle from 1913 to 1916. Stefansson organized and led the expedition. Originally, the National Geographic Society and the American Museum of Natural History intended to sponsor the expedition. However, Canada took over the sponsorship because of the potential for the discovery of a new continent. Stefansson selected Richard Bartlett as the captain of his ship due to his extensive experience in navigating the Arctic.

Although Captain Bartlett had concerns about the ability of the 29-year-old *Karluk* to navigate the Arctic ice, he accepted command of the ship. Stefansson planned to take the expedition to the old whaling station at Herschel Island, located near the Arctic Circle. The rush to meet the deadline set by the National Geographic Society led to concerns among the members of the expedition regarding the adequacy of the provision of food, clothing, and equipment.

The vessel departed British Columbia on June 17, 1913. The *Karluk* stopped in Nome to pick up dogs, and at Point Hope, to hire two Inupiaq hunters. At the Cape Smythe whaling station near Barrow, two more Alaska Native hunters, Kataktovik and Keraluk, came aboard, along with Keraluk's wife Keruk and their two young daughters, Helen and Mugpi.

The ship sailed eastward through increasingly heavy ice, but on August 13, it became permanently trapped about 235 miles east of Barrow and the same distance west of Herschel Island. In the following weeks, ocean currents pushed the ice and the ship back along the Alaskan coast. The vessel drifted helplessly with the pack ice, unable to break free. Although the group had enough food and shelter, it was clear that their survival depended on making their way to Wrangel Island, located off the Russian coast, in the direction they were being carried.

On September 10, the *Karluk* ship had to turn back towards Point Barrow after retreating nearly 100 miles from their original course. Shortly after, Stefansson informed Bartlett that further progress that year was not possible and *Karluk* would have to spend the winter on the ice. On September 19, realizing that they might face a long winter without meat, Stefansson decided to walk to the Colville River for caribou hunting. He was accompanied by two Point Hope hunters and several men from the expedition.

Stefansson never planned to return to the *Karluk*, as he was essentially abandoning the ship and members. On September 23, the speed of the *Karluk* drift increased dramatically. The ship began drifting westward at a rate of 30 to 60 miles per day captured in the ice floes. For weeks, Captain Bartlet repeatedly tried to free the ship from the ice but was unable to succeed.

On November 15, the sun dipped below the horizon and would not reappear until January. The ship's members would live in the dark ship, trying to survive the below-zero temperatures. Occasionally they would venture outside and observe the stars, seemingly so close you could almost touch them. The Arctic heavens offered a splendid spectacle of lunar coronas, lunar halos, and magnificent multicolored auroras, a lovely counterpoint to their bleak world.

The ship was drifting to the west and by the beginning of January the ship had traveled 50 miles to the north of Wrangel Island situated off the Siberian coast, and a positive sighting was made.

On January 10, 1914, the *Karluk's* hull was crushed by ice, causing it to sink. Fortunately, weeks earlier, Bartlett had ordered crewmembers to build igloos on the ice and transfer most of the ship's food, fuel, and other supplies to its surface in preparation for the sinking. As the *Karluk* slowly sank, the expedition members removed all remaining supplies and abandoned the ship. Bartlett stayed onboard until the last possible moment, playing dozens of records on the ship's Victrola. At about 3:30 p.m. on January 11, he placed Chopin's "Funeral March" on the turntable, stepped onto the ice, and watched the *Karluk* disappear below the water. Now, 22 men, one woman, two children, 16 dogs, and the ship's cat were stranded in the Arctic darkness, 50 miles from land.

Bartlett's decision to deposit stores on the ice ensured that an ice camp, known as "Shipwreck Camp," was established by the time *Karluk* sank. Two shelters had been built, one a snow igloo with a canvas roof, the other constructed from packing cases. Three small parties set off to search for land. Only Captain Bartlett's party successfully reached Wrangle Island civilization after a 700-mile journey.

In September 1914, which was more than a year after the ship got stuck, Bartlett returned to Alaska and made several attempts to rescue the survivors who were still stranded on the ice. However, all these attempts failed. Finally, the schooner *King & Winge* managed to reach the explorers who were stranded on the ice. Unfortunately, 11 out of the 31 members of the *Karluk* expedition had lost their lives.

Vilhjalmur Stefansson was chastised in the news for abandoning the expedition and leaving the *Karluk* stranded. Stefansson blamed Captain Bartlett for not navigating the ice properly. The populous regarded Captain Bartlett as a hero for saving the survivors.[135]

The expedition did discover new land, including the Brock, Mackenzie King, Borden, Meighen, Lougheed, and Stefansson Islands. The discovery produced valuable data and launched the careers of several explorers and scientists.

Chapter Thirteen
The *Matthew Turner* Tall Ship

The *Matthew Turner*, a 132-foot-long wooden ship, was constructed based on the design of the *Galilee*. This ship, in addition to meeting an environmental education need, also serves to represent the region's rich maritime and is the first tall ship built and launched in the San Francisco Bay Area in nearly 100 years. The total cost of the ship was $6.3 million dollars. This cost covered the construction of the vessel and the development of educational programs. Funds were received from individuals and foundations that share the values and support the mission. The *Matthew Turner* ship rolled down her launch ramp at the U.S. Army Corps of Engineers dock in Sausalito on Saturday, April 1, 2017.[136]

The *Matthew Turner* is the only operational educational tall ship based in the San Francisco Bay Area. With eleven sails, it offers a perfect opportunity to engage students in an exciting and meaningful hands-on experience. They must use team work and communicate well to power the ship safely. With the chance of going aloft into the rig to set and take in the square sails is a rite of passage and an experience that is never forgotten.

With scientists in agreement that marine diesel engines contribute a substantial amount of harmful pollutants to the environment, there was a crucial unmet need to develop more eco-friendly solutions for this industry. The project aimed to serve as a model of best practice for the sailing ship-building community. *Matthew Turner*'s innovative design allows the ship, when not propelled by wind, to be propelled by electric motors that draw energy from batteries instead of marine diesel engines. While under sail, energy generated from the propellers will charge the batteries. When the vessel is docked at the U.S. Army Corps of Engineers Bay Model pier (Call of the Sea's long-standing partner on this project) solar panels charge the propulsion system's batteries. In an additional sustainability measure, the ship was constructed using Forest Stewardship Certified lumber, with eighty percent of the timber coming from the Conservancy-funded Big River and Salmon Creek Forests, operated by The Conservation Fund.[137]

Figure 132: The *Matthew Turmer* tall ship.
Source: Call of the Sea.

Appendix A

List of ships designed and built by Matthew Turner

The list of vessels built by Matthew Turner was compiled from a number of sources:

- *Matthew Turner Foundation Ship List*, 10th revision, 1994.
- Lloyds Registry of Ships
- San Francisco Chamber of Commerce reports
- Various newspapers and magazines

Turner was required to complete a certificate of registration for all "large" vessels. This did not apply to smaller crafts (sloops, scows, fishing boats, lighters, etc.), drydocks, barges, dredges, and ships for personnel use. The Turner shipyards were well equipped with materials, equipment and labor such that they could turn around an order for a small vessel in rapid fashion.

The list in this appendix includes many smaller crafts, especially if the vessels were "named." Matthew Turner built 265 vessels in his career as a shipbuilder at six different locations.

- Geneva on Indian Creek, Ohio (1).
- Euphronius B. Cousins Island Shipyard, Eureka, California (4).
- Cutten & McDonald's Shipyard, Eureka, California (2).
- B. F. Webster Shipyard, Mission Bay, San Francisco (1).
- Turner Shipyard, Mission Bay, San Francisco (73).
- Turner Shipyard, Benicia California (184).

Column information for Appeendix A is as follows:

- The year is the date launched.
- Tonnage is a measure of a ship's overall internal volume (not for cargo).
- LOD is the length of the deck in feet.
- The beam is the width of the ship in feet.
- Draft is the vertical distance between the waterline and the bottom of the hull (keel).
- Schooners are 2-masted unless otherwise indicated.
- Aux or auxiliary, meaning a secondary source of power.
- Screw indicates a propeller design.

	Name	Date	Type, Tonnage, LOD	Shipyard	Original Owner
1.	*George R. Roberts*	1848	Schooner, 75 tons	Geneva Indian Creek	Matthew Turner
2.	*Nautilus*	1868 Nov 18	Half-brigantine, 260 tons, 115' LOD, 26' beam, 10.6' draft	E.B Cousins Shipyard Eureka, CA	Matthew Turner
3.	*Island Belle* [138]	1871 Jan 19	Schooner, 41.86 tons, 66' LOD, 15' beam	B. F. Webster Shipyard, Mission Bay San Francisco	Tahiti trade
4.	*Stella* [139]	1872 Feb 1	Schooner, 49 tons, 75' LOD, 20.6' beam, 6' draft	Cutten & McDonald's Shipyard Eureka, CA	Tahiti trade
5.	*Marion* [140]	1872 July 10	Schooner, 48 tons, 75' LOD, 20.6' beam, 6' draft	E.B Cousins Shipyard Eureka, CA	Tahiti trade
6.	*Mary* [141]	1872 Nov 23	Schooner, 49 tons, 123' LOD, 31.8' beam	Cutten & McDonald's Shipyard Eureka, CA	Tahiti trade
7.	*Atalanta* [142]	1872 Dec 27	Schooner, 49 tons	E.B Cousins Shipyard Eureka, CA	Tahiti trade
8.	*Francaise* [143]	1874 Nov 1	Schooner, 70 tons	E.B Cousins Shipyard Eureka, CA	French Polynesia
9.	*Siberia* [144]	1875 March	Brigantine, steam-screw, 126 tons, 74' LOD, 23' beam	B. F. Webster Shipyard Mission Bay San Francisco	Lindholm & Co. Vladivostok, Russia
10.	*Alata*	1875 May 4	Schooner, 60 tons	Mission Bay San Francisco	Turner, Chapman & Co. Hawaii
11.	*Marie*	1875 May 4	Schooner, 25 tons	Mission Bay San Francisco	John Pinet, Tahiti trade
12.	*Mabel Scott*	1875 July 22	Schooner, 76.6 tons, 81.7' LOD, 22.7' beam, 7.8' draft	Mission Bay San Francisco	Turner & Rundle, Tahiti trade
13.	*Namalole*	1875	Schooner, 59 tons	Mission Bay San Francisco	Benj Greaves
14.	*Theodore H. Allen*	1875 Sept 15	Schooner, pilot, 48.31 tons, 67.5' LOD, 20' beam, 8' draft	Mission Bay San Francisco	San Francisco Bar Pilots
15.	*Colorado*	1875 Oct 18	Sloop, 20 tons, 47' LOD, 15.5' beam, 5.3' draft	Mission Bay San Francisco	Commodore Isadore Gutte
16.	*Eudora*	1876 Mar 15	Schooner, 73 tons, 80' LOD, 22.4' beam, 8' draft	Mission Bay San Francisco	Alaska Commercial Company

17.	*Bella*	1876 Mar 15	Schooner, 34 tons, 58' LOD, 34.8' beam, 5.3' draft	Mission Bay San Francisco	Alaska Commercial Company
18.	*Dagmar*	1876 March	Schooner, 60 tons, 79' LOD, 22.8' beam, 6.5' draft	Mission Bay San Francisco	Hutchinson & Co. Petropavlovsk, Russia
19.	*Salvatierre*	1876 Apr 14	Schooner, 64.19 tons, 79' LOD, 22.8' beam, 5.5' draft	Mission Bay San Francisco	Commodore Isadore Gutte
20.	*Unga*	1876 July 22	Schooner, 24 tons, 48.5 LOD, 16.5' beam, 5.6' draft	Mission Bay San Francisco	T. W. McCollum
21.	*Nagay*	1876 July 22	Schooner, 20.19 tons, 48.5' LOD, 16.5' beam, 5.6' draft	Mission Bay San Francisco	T. W. McCollum
22.	*Lalla Rookh*[145]	1876 Sept 2	Schooner, yacht, 59' LOD, 18' beam, 4.5' draft	Mission Bay San Francisco	Governor Romualdo Pacheco
23.	*Pearl*[146]	1876 Sept	Schooner yacht, 60' LOD, 18' beam, 4.5' draft	Mission Bay San Francisco	Commodore John L. Eckley
24.	*Alexander*	1877 Feb 27	Schooner, 52.12 tons, 58' LOD, 22' beam, 7.2' draft	Mission Bay San Francisco	Liebes Brothers, San Francisco
25.	*Consuelo*	1877 Sept 2	Schooner, yacht, 25.64 tons, 56' LOD, 18' beam, 4.25' draft	Mission Bay San Francisco	Commodore Isadore Gutte
26.	*Haleakala*	1877 Oct 1	Schooner, 55 tons, 75' LOD, 23' beam, 8' draft	Mission Bay San Francisco	Allen & Robinson, Hawaii
27.	*Matthew Turner*[147]	1877 Nov 20	Schooner, 75.03 tons, 85' LOD, 23' beam, 7.1' draft	Mission Bay San Francisco	Commodore Isadore Gutte
28.	*Vladimir*	1878 Feb 16	Schooner, steam-aux, 71.03 tons, 77' LOD, 21.7' beam, 7' draft	Mission Bay San Francisco	Lindholm & Co. Vladivostok, Russia
29.	*Leon*	1878 Apr 10	Schooner, 67.41 tons, 76' LOD, 21.2' beam, 7.3' draft	Mission Bay San Francisco	Alaska Commercial Company
30.	*Marguerita*	1878 Apr 24	Sloop yacht, 20.21 tons, 53' LOD, 15' beam, 4.5' draft	Mission Bay San Francisco	Commodore Isadore Gutte
31.	*Rosario*	1878 May 2	Schooner, 148.65 tons, 99' LOD, 26.6' beam, 9' draft	Mission Bay San Francisco	Lewis L. Bradburry & Co. San Francisco
32.	*Ester Cobos*	1878 June 1	Schooner scow, 58.21 tons, 72' LOD, 22' beam, 5.3' draft	Mission Bay San Francisco	Carroll & Co. San Francisco

33.	*St. George*	1878 July 13	Schooner, 100.41 tons, 91' LOD, 24.7' beam, 8.3' draft	Mission Bay San Francisco	Alaska Commercial Company
34.	*Flora*	1878 Aug 18	Schooner, 44 tons	Mission Bay San Francisco	Papeete, Tahiti
35.	*Rescue*	1878 Aug 27	Schooner, pilot, 70.46 tons, 78' LOD, 22.8' beam, 7.2' draft, price $8,000	Mission Bay San Francisco	Columbia River Bar Pilots, Astoria, Washington
36.	*Lillian*	1878 Oct 9	Schooner, 70 tons	Mission Bay San Francisco	Johnsen, Tahiti
37.	*St. Paul* [148]	1879 Feb 1	Steamer, 26' LOD	Mission Bay San Francisco	Alaska Commercial Company
38.	*Ounalaska*	1879 April 14	Schooner, 54.42 tons, 70' LOD, 22.2' beam, 6.8' draft	Mission Bay San Francisco	Western Fur and Trading Co.
39.	*Claus Spreckels*	1879 June 12	Brigantine, 246.62 tons, 122.5' LOD, 31.8' beam, 10.5' draft	Mission Bay San Francisco	John D. Spreckels Oceanic S.S. Co.
40.	*La Mangarevienne*	1879 June 25	Schooner, 72 tons	Mission Bay San Francisco	French Polynesia
41.	*Dolly*	1879 July 13	Schooner, 42 tons	Mission Bay San Francisco	Stephen Higgins, Tahiti
42.	*Chispa*	1879 July 26	Schooner, yacht, 30.73 tons, 56.6' LOD, 18.6' beam, 4.9' draft	Mission Bay San Francisco	Commodore Isador Gutte
43.	*Nellie*	1879 Oct 11	Sloop, yacht, 14.37 tons, 43.7' LOD, 15.3' beam, 3.5' draft	Mission Bay San Francisco	Hyde R. Bowie, San Francisco
44.	*John D. Spreckels*	1880 Feb 14	Half-brigantine, 266.66 tons, 124.6' LOD, 31.2' beam, 10.9' draft	Mission Bay San Francisco	John D. Spreckels Oceanic S.S. Co.
45.	*Dora*	1880 Apr 2	Brigantine, steam-screw, 198 tons, 112' LOD, 27.2' beam, 13.2' draft	Mission Bay San Francisco	Alaska Commercial Company
46.	*Punau*	1880 Apr 2	Schooner, 42 tons	Mission Bay San Francisco	Tahiti
47.	*Consuelo*	1880 July 23	Half-brigantine, 293.54 tons, 133.5' LOD, 31.2' beam, 11.7' draft	Mission Bay San Francisco	John D. Spreckels Oceanic S.S. Co.
48.	*Ella*	1880 Oct 2	Schooner, 43 tons	Mission Bay San Francisco	Johanson & Co. Tahiti
49.	*Nellie* [149]	1880 Oct 2	Sloop yacht, 32 tons, 60' LOD	Mission Bay San Francisco	Hyde R. Bowie, San Francisco

50.	*Lotus*	1880 Nov 24	Schooner, 40 tons, 68' LOD, 16.6' beam, 5.3' draft	Mission Bay San Francisco	F. J. Jackson, San Francisco
51.	*W. H. Dimond*	1881 Jan 20	Barkentine, 390.59 tons, 155' LOD, 35.5' beam, 11.75' draft	Mission Bay San Francisco	John D. Spreckels Oceanic S.S. Co
52.	*Czar*	1881 Feb 10	Schooner, 144.34 tons, 98' LOD, 26' beam, 97.5' draft	Mission Bay San Francisco	Western Fur Trading Co.
53.	*Otter*	1881 Feb 15	Schooner, 73.75 tons, 81' LOD, 24.6' beam, 7.6' draft	Mission Bay San Francisco	H. Liebes, San Francisco
54.	*Nuku Hiva*	1881 Mar 16	Schooner, 75 tons, 72' LOD, 24.2' beam, 6' draft	Mission Bay San Francisco	French Government
55.	*Taravao*	1881 Apr 3	Schooner, 75 tons, 72' LOD, 24.2' beam, 6' draft	Mission Bay San Francisco	France Government
56.	*Anna*	1881 Apr 16	Schooner, 239.46 tons, 117' LOD, 29.5' beam, 10.6' draft	Mission Bay San Francisco	John D. Spreckels Oceanic S.S. Co.
57.	*William G. Irwin*	1881 June 10	Half-brigantine, 348.16 tons, 135' LOD, 32.9' beam, 13' draft	Mission Bay San Francisco	John D. Spreckels Oceanic S.S. Co.
58.	*Kodiak*	1881 June 28	Schooner, 103 tons, 93' LOD, 25' beam, 8.2' draft	Mission Bay San Francisco	Alaska Commercial Company
59.	*Tahiti*	1881 Aug 18	Half-brigantine, 290 tons, 124' LOD, 32.3' beam, 12' draft	Mission Bay San Francisco	Turner & Rundle, San Francisco
60.	*City of San Diego*	1881 Aug 23	Schooner, 48.58 tons, 67.5' LOD, 20.5' beam, 6.5' draft	Mission Bay San Francisco	E. Daily & Co. San Francisco
61.	*Poor Beggar*	1881	Sloop, yacht, 25.5' LOD	Mission Bay San Francisco	Matthew Turner's Shipyard Boat
62.	*Emma Claudina*	1882 Mar 28	Schooner, 3-masted, 195.65 tons, 113' LOD, 31.5' beam, 8.7' draft	Mission Bay San Francisco	Spreckels Bros. Captain William Matson
63.	*J.C. Ford*	1882 May 5	Schooner, 3-masted, 243.66 tons, 123' LOD, 31.8' beam, 10.3' draft	Mission Bay San Francisco	J. C. Ford and Company
64.	*Josephine*	1882 May 14	Schooner, 64.22 tons, 77.5' LOD, 22' beam, 7.3' draft	Mission Bay San Francisco	Hale & Company, San Francisco
65.	*Garcia*	1882 June 17	Schooner, 110.61 tons, 94' LOD, 24.5' beam, 7.5' draft	Mission Bay San Francisco	S. B. Peterson San Francisco

66.	*Canute*	1882 July 14	Schooner, 118.89 tons, 92.5' LOD, 27.2' beam, 7.5' draft	Mission Bay San Francisco	J. N. Pedlar, San Francisco
67.	*Vigaronne*	1882 July	Schooner, 140' LOD, 34' beam, 10' draft	Mission Bay San Francisco	B.C. Genereaux France
68.	*Eva*	1882 Aug 31	Schooner, 4.55 tons, 63.5 LOD, 20.4' beam	Mission Bay San Francisco	J. Kentfield & Company
69.	*Marion*	1882 Aug 21	Schooner, 235.66 tons, 123' LOD, 31.8' beam, 10.3' draft	Mission Bay San Francisco	Oliver Smith & Co. San Francisco
70.	*George H. Ross*	1882 Aug 31	Schooner, 30.45 tons, 56' LOD, 18' beam, 5.7' draft	Mission Bay San Francisco	George H. Ross
71.	*Lurline*	1882 Oct 25	Schooner yacht, 47.25 tons, 75' LOD, 21.2' beam, 6.9' draft	Mission Bay San Francisco	J.D. Spreckels Matson Lines
72.	*Cometa*	1882 Nov 18	Schooner, 80.49 tons, 95' LOD, 23.1' beam, 7.3' draft	Mission Bay San Francisco	Commodore Isadore Gutte
73.	*Vesta*	1882 Dec 5	Schooner, 3-masted, 272.59 tons, 127.8' LOD, 32' beam, 10' draft	Mission Bay San Francisco	B.C. Genereaux France
74.	*Selina*	1883 Jan 22	Half-brigantine, 331.99 tons, 135' LOD, 33' beam, 11.4' draft	Mission Bay San Francisco	Shipping Company of Portland
75.	*Theresa*	1883 Feb	Schooner, scow, 70 tons	Mission Bay San Francisco	Celia P. Lewis
76.	*Papeete*	1883 Mar 8	Schooner, 49.69 tons, 66.5' LOD, 20' beam, 6.5' draft	Mission Bay San Francisco	Turner & Chapman Company Tahiti
77.	*Sea Witch*	1883 Mar 10	Tug, steam, 74.12 tons, 77.9' LOD, 20' beam, 10' draft	Mission Bay San Francisco	Merchants Tugboat Company, San Francisco
78.	*Tuamotu*	1883 Mar 11	Schooner, 40.45 tons, 66.6' LOD, 20' beam, 6.6' draft	Mission Bay San Francisco	Wilkens & C0. German Registry
79.	*Ahome*	1883 May 21	Schooner, 21.06 tons, 53' LOD, 15,3' beam, 5.1' draft	Mission Bay San Francisco	Thanhauser & Company
80.	*Norma*[150]	1883 May	Schooner, 3-masted, 326.3 tons, 138.5' LOD, 34.1' beam, 10.5' draft	Mission Bay San Francisco	Russ Lumber Company
81.	*Alert*	1883 June 5	Tug, steam, 35.6 tons, 78' LOD, 19.5' beam, 9.8' draft	Mission Bay San Francisco	John D. Spreckels

#	Name	Date	Description	Location	Owner
82.	*Amethyst*	1883 July 17	Schooner, 70.56 tons, 72.5' LOD, 26' beam, 5.7' draft	Benicia	Captain Merrill, San Francisco
83.	*Hawaiiland*	1883 Sept 19	Schooner, 40 tons	Benicia	Hawaii
84.	*Nassau*	1883 Oct 26	Schooner, 37.74 tons, 64' LOD, 18.5' beam, 6' draft	Benicia	Ellacott Company, San Francisco
85.	*Courtney Ford*	1883 Nov 14	Half-brigantine, 480 tons, 146.3' LOD, 34.2' beam, 12.5' draft	Benicia	J. J. McKinnon Lumber Company, San Francsico
86.	*Monotambo*	1883	Schooner	Benicia	French Polynesia
87.	*Islander*	1883	Schooner, scow	Benicia	Unknown
88.	*Henrietta*	1884 Feb 14	Schooner, 44.26 tons, 61.4' LOD, 20.1' beam, 6.5' draft	Benicia	Captain James Sennate & Co.
89.	*Karluk*	1884 Mar 15	Half-brigantine, steam screw, 202.57 tons, 125.6' LOD, 27' beam, 14.2' draft	Benicia	Karluk Packing Company
90.	*Jennie Griffin*	1884 Mar 26	Schooner, 16.86 tons. 46.4' LOD, 16.3' beam, 4.4' draft	Benicia	R. G. Gibson San Francisco
91.	Unknown Name	1884 Apr 16	Schooner, 50 tons	Benicia	Unknown
92.	*Cecilia*	1884 Apr 18	Schooner, 3-masted, steam, 115.50 tons, 115' LOD, 29' beam, 8.6' draft	Benicia	George H. Collins, San Francisco
93.	*Nellie* [151]	1884 Apr 27	Schooner, yacht, 32 tons	Benicia	Peter J. Donahue San Francisco
94.	*Resolute*	1884 May 5	Steamer, stern-wheel, 242.66 tons, 134' LOD, 29' beam, 5.5' draft	Benicia	Spreckels Refinery San Francisco
95.	*Celia* [152]	1884 June	Steamer, 215' LOD, 29.5' beam, 12' draft	Benicia	Higgins & Collins San Francisco
96.	*Lizzie Merrill*	1884 June 6	Schooner, 54.68 tons, 69' LOD, 23' beam, 5.9' draft	Benicia	Lewis Merrill & others
97.	*Jennie & Edna*	1884 June 19	Schooner, 63 tons, 70' LOD, 24' beam, 5.5' draft	Benicia	Mr. Norden
98.	*Porfirio Diaz*	1884 July 23	Schooner, steam screw, 27.74 tons	Benicia	Juan Hidalgo Mexico
99.	*Garnet* [153]	1884 Sept 25	Steamer, 30' LOD, 7' beam, 5' draft	Benicia	Commodore John L. Eckley
100.	Unknown name	1885 Jan	Schooner, 60' LOD	Benicia	French Registry Tahiti
101.	*Alert* [154]	1885 Jan 20	Tug, steam, 37.68 tons, 86' LOD, 20' beam, 9.5' draft	Benicia	John D. Spreckels

102.	James A. Hamilton	1885 Jan 20	Schooner, 73.91 tons, 81.5' LOD, 24' beam, 7.5' draft	Benicia	Magee, Moore & Company San Francisco
103.	Peru	1885 Feb 14	Steamer, 42' LOD, 10' beam, 5' draft	Benicia	Peruvian Registry
104.	Azteca	1885 Feb 19	Schooner, 45 tons, 72' LOD, 20' beam, 6' draft	Benicia	Mexican owners, Mazatlán
105.	Ondina [155]	1885 Mar 29	Sloop, 31.90 tons, 70' LOD, 18' beam, 5.25' draft	Benicia	Altata, Mexico
106.	Emma	1885 Apr 17	Schooner, 42.91 tons, 68.8' LOD, 20' beam, 6.5' draft	Benicia	Mexican owners
107.	James I. Dawsett [156]	1885 Apr 29	Schooner, steam screw, 100 tons, 98' LOD, 20' beam, 8' draft	Benicia	F. Wandenberger, Inter-Island Steam Navigation Co.
108.	Solano	1885 May 23	Schooner, scow, 63.24 tons, 54' LOD, 22' beam, 5.5' draft, price $7,000	Benicia	Piper, Aden, & Goodall Company, San Francisco
109.	Navigator	1885 June 6	Schooner, 42.49 tons, 61' LOD, 18.5' beam, 6.3' draft, Price $10,000	Benicia	Wightman Brothers
110.	Gracie B. Richardson	1885 June 8	Schooner, 59.45 tons, 70' LOD, 23.5' beam, 6.3' draft	Benicia	Capt. Sandberg, San Francisco
111.	John Rodgers	1885 June 22	Steamer, 60' LOD, 18' beam, 5' draft	Benicia	US Army Benicia Arsenal
112.	Domatilla	1885 Aug 29	Schooner	Benicia	Hawaiian registry
113.	M. Romero Rubio	1885 Nov 28	Schooner, steam-aux, 60 tons	Benicia	International Company of Mexico
114.	San Jose	1886 Mar 11	Schooner, 51.88 tons, 67.5' LOD, 20' beam, 7' draft	Benicia	James Girvan, San Francisco
115.	Reliance	1886 Apr 1	Schooner, 61.34 tons, 69.5' LOD, 23' beam, 6.5' draft	Benicia	Henry Steffens San Francisco
116.	Frank Lawrence	1886 Apr 9	Schooner, scow, 55.76 tons, 63' LOD, 24' beam, 4.5' draft	Benicia	Frank Lawrence, San Francisco
117.	Pearl	1886 Apr 9	Schooner, 83.56 tons, 95.5' LOD, 23' beam, 7.5' draft	Benicia	Louis Sloss, San Francisco
118.	Moe Wahine	1886 May 21	Schooner, 60 tons, 85' LOD, 24' beam, 9' draft	Benicia	Hawaiian Registry
119.	Mateata	1886 July 19	Schooner, 50.73 tons, 67.1' LOD, 20.4' beam, 7' draft	Benicia	A. Crawford San Francisco

120.	*Apia*[157]	1886 Aug 10	Schooner, 53.4 tons. 67.1' LOD', 20.4" beam, 7' draft	Benicia	Wightman Brothers
121.	*Lovina*	1886 Dec 7	Schooner, 67.67 tons, 73.5' LOD, 22.5' beam, 8' draft	Benicia	Matthew Turner & Company Tahiti
122.	*Berwick*	1887 Jan 20	Schooner, 95.67 tons, 82.6' LOD, 27.4 beam, 7.1' draft, price $7,700	Benicia	R. D. Hume Del Norte Commercial Co.
123.	*Del Norte*	1887 Feb 2	Schooner, 95.64 tons. 82.6' LOD, 27.4' beam, 7.1' draft, price $7,700	Benicia	R. D. Hume Del Norte Commercial Co.
124.	*Chetco*	1887 Mar 8	Schooner, 98.69 tons, 83.6' LOD, 27.4' beam, 7.2' draft, price $8,000	Benicia	R. D. Hume Del Norte Commercial Co.
125.	*Thistle*[158]	1887 Apr 20	Whaleback steam tug, 32.38 tons, 72' LOD, 18' beam, 10' draft, price $11,800	Benicia	R. D. Hume
126.	*Nellie*[159]	1887 April	Schooner, yacht, 88' LOD, 21' beam, 10.3' draft	Benicia	J. Mervyn Donahue San Francisco
127.	*Antelope*[160]	1887 May 27	Schooner, 123,98 tons, 89.5' LOD, 28.8' beam, 7' draft	Benicia	G. W. Hume, San Francisco
128.	*Lurline*	1887 June 2	Half-brigantine, 350 tons, 135' LOD, 34.4' beam, 13' draft, price $26,000	Benicia	J.D Spreckels Oceanic S.S. Co.
129.	*Eureka*	1887 June 27	Schooner, 117.77 tons, 89.5' LOD,28.5' beam, 7' draft, price $9,000	Benicia	L. A Maison, San Francisco
130.	*Elsie Iverson*	1887 Aug 6	Schooner, 116.23 tons, 93.5' LOD, 27.2' beam, 7.5' draft, price $10,500	Benicia	Nils Iverson
131.	*Newark*	1887 Sept 1	Schooner, 114.53 tons, 93.5' LOD, 27.2' beam, 7.2' draft, price $11,000	Benicia	C.L. Dingley
132.	*Monterey*	1887 Oct 6	Schooner, 119.84 tons, 96.5' LOD, 28' beam, 7.5' draft, price $11,000	Benicia	C.L. Dingley
133.	*Confianza*	1888 Jan 14	Schooner, 84.23 tons, 78' LOD, 25.5' beam, 7' draft	Benicia	Henry Topfer
134.	*Fruto*	1888 Jan	Steamer, stern-wheel, 429 tons, 235' LOD, 45' beam, 5.6' draft	Benicia	Freeman, Smith & Company Russian Registry
135.	*Seven Sisters*	1888 Mar 3	Schooner, 122.81 tons, 97' LOD, 27.2' beam, 7.5' draft, price $12,000	Benicia	Shattuck & Co.
136.	*Bertha*	1888 Apr 12	Half-brigantine steam-aux, 449 tons, 140' LOD, 32' beam, 15' draft, price $32,000	Benicia	Karluk Packing Company

137.	*Alice*	1888	Steamer, stern-wheel	Benicia	Pacific Packing & Navigation Co. Sitka, Alaska
138.	*Equator*	1888 May 31	Schooner, 72,68 tons, 66.5' LOD, 22' beam, 8' draft	Benicia	K. C. Eldridge, Pacific Packing & Navigation Co. San Francisco
139.	*Portia*	1888 June 19	Schooner, 62.88 tons, 75' LOD, 23' beam, 6' draft	Benicia	Higgins & Collins Lumber Company, San Francisco
140.	*America*	1888 July 21	Schooner, pilot, 74.74 tons, 81' LOD, 24' beam, 9.7' draft, price $20,000	Benicia	San Francisco Bar Pilots
141.	*Cudina*	1888	Schooner	Benicia	Unknown
142.	*Helene*	1889 Jan 25	Schooner, yacht, 40' LOD, 18' beam, 5' draft	Benicia	Col. Fred Whitney Hawaii
143.	*Linda*	1889 Jan	Sloop, yacht, 9 tons, 36.9 LOD, 14' beam, 5.5' draft	Benicia	Judge Prescott Sawyer
144.	Unknown	1889 Jan	Tug, steam, sub-assembled and shipped to Alaska	Benicia	Alaska Commercial Company
145.	*Lydia*	1889 Apr 1	Schooner, 39 tons, 62' LOD, 20' Beam, 7' draft	Benicia	Karluk Packing Company
146.	*Jennie*	1889 Mar 7	Schooner, steam-screw, 50.75 tons, 72.9' LOD, 22' beam, 7' draft	Benicia	Alaska Commercial Company
147.	*Aleut*	1889 Mar 7	Schooner, steam-screw, 19.17 tons, 59.5' LOD, 19'beam, 7' draft	Benicia	Alaska Commercial Company
148.	*Pinole*	1889 Apr 27	Schooner, 77.56 tons, 72' LOD, 25.4' beam, 6.5' draft	Benicia	Sacramento Farm Hay Vessel
149.	*Arthur I.*	1889 May 17	Schooner, 129.26 tons, 97' LOD, 27.3' beam, 7.7' draft, price $12,000	Benicia	Nils Iverson, Iverson & Co. Benicia
150.	*Volcano*	1889 May	Sloop, yacht, 13.38 tons, 27' LOD	Benicia	German Registration
151.	*Molly Woggin*	1889 June	Sloop, yacht, 27' LOD	Benicia	Matthew Turner
152.	*Arctic*	1889 Aug 4	Steamer, stern-wheel, 42.07 tons, 60.6' LOD, 19' beam, 7' draft, Sub-assembled and shipped to Alaska	Benicia	Alaska Commercial Company
153.	*Reliance*	1889 Sept 24	Schooner, steam-screw, 94.21 tons, 92.9' LOD, 21.2' beam, 10.5' draft	Benicia	John D. Spreckels, San Francisco
153.	*Eva*	1889	Schooner, 36.87 tons, 64" LOD, 22.3'beam, 3.3' draft	Benicia	Unknown

155.	*Olga*	1890 Jan 13	Schooner, 46.12 tons, 63.5' LOD, 20' beam, 7' draft	Benicia	Captain Boden
156.	*Herman*	1890 Feb 14	Schooner, 105.75 tons, 87.5' LOD, 24.5' beam, 10' draft	Benicia	George Liebes Fur Company
157.	*St. Paul*	1890 Mar 28	Schooner, 46.14 tons, 63.5' LOD, 20' beam, 7' draft	Benicia	M. L. Washburne Kodiak, Alaska
158.	*Pacific*	1890 Apr 14	Schooner, steam-screw, 31.66 tons, 75' LOD, 20.6' beam, 8.2' draft	Benicia	Leon Sloss Pacific Packing Co.
158.	*Archie & Fontie*	1890 May 20	Schooner, 61.28 tons, 76.5' LOD, 25.5' beam, 6.3' draft	Benicia	Captain H. A. Richardson
160.	*Mikronesia*	1890 June 4	Schooner, 35 tons, 60' LOD, 16' beam, 6' draft	Benicia	A.G. Jaluit-Gesellschaft, Hamburg
161.	*Emma*	1890 June 16	Schooner, 25.33 tons, 51.5' LOD, 16.8' beam, 6' draft	Benicia	Captain Brown Benson Margovia, Alaska
162.	*Jessie*	1890 June	Schooner, yacht, 76 tons, 76' LOD, 24.5' beam, 8.7' draft	Benicia	Commodore Joseph MacDonough San Francisco
163.	*Pitcairn*	1890 July 28	Schooner, yacht, 121.52 tons, 93.5' LOD, 27.2' beam, 10' draft, price $18,683	Benicia	O. Oleen. San Francisco, Seventh-day Adventists
164.	*Ramona*	1890 Aug 1	Schooner, yacht, 31.50 tons, 58.5' LOD, 19.6' beam, 6.5' draft	Benicia	J. H. McCarthy, San Francisco
165.	*Glad Tidings* [161]	1890 Aug 15	Steamer, price $35,000	Benicia	Second Adventist Church
166.	*Robert W. Logan*	1890 Aug 29	Schooner, 28.62 tons, 53' LOD, 17.5' beam, 7' draft	Benicia	American Board of Foreign Missions of Boston
167.	*Alister* [162]	1890 Aug 30	Schooner, 80 tons, 80' LOD, 23 ½' beam, 8' draft	Benicia	A.G. Jaluit-Gesellschaft, Hamburg
168.	*Northern*	1890	Schooner, steam screw	Benicia	Unknown
169.	*Galilee*	1891 Feb 8	Half-brigantine, 354.07 tons, 132.5" LOD, 33.5' beam, 12.7' draft	Benicia	Matthew Turner
170.	*Royal*	1891 Mar 7	Schooner, steam-aux, 29.54 tons, 75' LOD, 20.6' beam, 8.2' draft	Benicia	Royal Packing Company

171.	*Benicia*	1891 Apr 22	Schooner, scow, 30.88 tons, 49.6' LOD, 20.2' beam, 4' draft	Benicia	Albert Eriksen San Francisco
172.	*La Tahitienne*	1891 June 20	Schooner, 82.33 tons, 106' LOD, 21.9' beam, 7' draft	Benicia	Mr. Emile Levy French Registry
173.	*Teavaroa*	1891 July 25	Schooner, 110 tons, 89' LOD, 28' beam, 8' draft	Benicia	Tahiti owners
174.	*Henry*	1891 July 29	Schooner, 50 tons, 81' LOD, 21.9' beam, 7' draft, $7,920	Benicia	Société Comm. de l'Océanie, Hamburg
175.	*Churruca*	1891 Oct	Schooner, 50 tons	Benicia	Mexican owners
176.	*Truant*[163]	1891	Sloop, yacht, 30' LOD	Benicia	Corinthian Yacht Club
177.	*Hunter*	1892 Mar 11	Schooner, 63.32 tons, 75' LOD, 26.6' beam, 7' draft	Benicia	Rudolph Neumann Ounalaska, Alaska
178.	*Papeete*	1892 Feb 12	Schooner, 127 tons, 112' LOD, 33.4' beam, 11.8' draft	Benicia	French Government Gunboat
179.	*Rachel*	1892 Apr 11	Schooner, 84.47 tons, 79.5' LOD, 25.7' beam, 6.7' draft, price $8,000	Benicia	Naval Reserve Company D
180.	*Hiawatha*	1892 Apr 20	Steamer, 9.78 tons, 125 HP, 49' LOD, 13' beam, 6' draft	Benicia	Commodore John Eckley, Eckley Station, Contra Costa County
181.	*Everett Hays*	1892 Apr 20	Schooner, 37.07 tons, 60' LOD, 19.2 beam, 6' draft	Benicia	Samuel Applegate Ounalaska, Alaska
182.	*Shasta*	1892 June 6	Schooner, scow, 91.17 tons, 82' LOD, 26' beam, 6.1' draft	Benicia	Piper, Aden & Company
183.	*Alpine*	1892 June 23	Schooner, scow. 91.17 tons, 82' LOD, 26' beam, 6.1' draft	Benicia	Piper, Aden & Company
184.	*Geneva*	1892 Dec 9	Half-brigantine, 495.66 tons, 150' LOD, 36.3' beam, 14' draft	Benicia	Nelson Andrews Matthew Turner & Company
185.	*Joseph & Henry*	1892 Aug 1	Schooner, 90.01 tons, 84' LOD, 27' beam, 6.6' draft	Benicia	Joseph Harder & Henry Stefffens San Francisco
186.	*Naiad*[164]	1893 July 15	Yawl, yacht	Benicia	Fred Kelley
187.	*Jeanette*	1893 Feb 18	Half-brigantine, steam-aux, 217.81 tons, 116' LOD, 27.2' beam, 13.2' draft	Benicia	Roth, Blum & Co. San Francisco
188.	*Santa Cruz*	1893 May 5	Schooner, 43.40 tons, 64' LOD, 18.8' beam, 6.4' draft	Benicia	Santa Cruz Island Co.

189.	*Tulenkun*	1893 June 1	Schooner, 47.07 tons, 61' LOD, 19.5' beam, 6.5' draft	Benicia	A.G. Jaluit-Gesellschaft, Hamburg
190.	*Tolna*	1893 July 19	Schooner, yacht, 78.61 tons, 88' LOD, 24.5' beam, 10' draft	Benicia	Count Festetics von Tolna
191.	*Benack* [165]	1894 Aug 21	Schooner, 53 tons	Benicia	A.G. Jaluit-Gesellschaft, Hamburg
192.	*Anita*	1894 Dec 27	Schooner, 83.71 tons, 82' LOD, 24.3' beam, 6.2' draft	Benicia	W. F. Boole & Co. Ybarra Mining Co.
193.	*Dry Dock*	1895 Mar 9	301-foot long capacity dry dock	Benicia	California Drydock Company San Francisco
194.	*Etta B.*	1895 Mar 27	Schooner, gas screw, 27.83 tons, 51' LOD, 18' beam, 4.9' draft	Benicia	C. Matsen Bolinas, California
195.	*Ida A.*	1895 Apr 3	Schooner, 26.6 tons, 53' LOD, 16.4' beam, 5.4' draft	Benicia	Thomas Marshall San Francisco
196.	*Alice* [166]	1895 May 23	Steamer, stern-wheel, 400 tons, 160' LOD, 30' beam, 9' draft, Sub-assembled and shipped to Alaska	Benicia	Pacific Packing & Navigation Co. Sitka, Alaska
197.	*Beaver* [167]	1895 May 24	Steamer, stern-wheel, 37 tons, 59' LOD, 15' beam, 3.1' draft, Sub-assembled and shipped to Alaska	Benicia	Pacific Packing & Navigation Co. Sitka, Alaska
198.	*Four Sisters*	1895 June 8	Schooner, gas-screw, 31.54 tons, 58.5' LOD, 20.6' beam, 4.5' draft	Benicia	J. P. Hauto Sonoma State
199.	*Kodiak*	1895 Aug 6	Schooner, 125.28 tons, 105' LOD, 25.3' beam, 9.3' draft	Benicia	Alaska Commercial Company
200.	*Gertrude*	1895 Dec 13	Sloop, 6.65 tons, 25.5' LOD, 11.7' beam, 2.9' draft	Benicia	Unknown
201.	*Gerald C.*	1895 Dec 29	Schooner, gas-screw, 75 tons, 68' LOD, 18' beam, 5.2' draft, price $6,000	Benicia	Frank Cooley Ravenswood, CA
202.	*Five Brothers*	1896 Mar 11	Schooner, steam-aux, 70.44 tons, 79' LOD, 25.7'beam, 6.4' draft	Benicia	Johnsen & Emigh, San Francisco
203.	*Baranoff*	1896 Mar 13	Schooner, steam-aux, 57.24 tons, 74.5' LOD, 22.7' beam, 7.6' draft	Benicia	Alaska Commercial Company
204.	*Maksoutoff*	1896 Mar 13	Schooner, 57.24 tons, 74.5' LOD, 22.7' beam, 7.6' draft	Benicia	Alaska Commercial Company

205.	*Bella*	1896	Steamer, stern-wheel, 400 HP, 370 tons, 140' LOD, 33' beam, 8' draft, Sub-assembled and shipped to Alaska	Benicia	Northern Commercial Co. St Michaels, Alaska
206.	*Rover*	1896	Schooner, yacht, 76 tons. 76' LOD, 22.7' beam, 9.6' draft	Benicia	R. Barrett Fithian
207.	*Duxbury*	1896 Aug 3	Schooner, gas auxiliary, 30.95 tons, 61.5 LOD, 19' beam, 5.1' draft	Benicia	George L. Gibson Bolinas, California
208.	*Mercur*	1896 Oct	Schooner, 52 tons, 70' LOD, 20' beam, 7' draft	Benicia	A.G. Jaluit-Gesellschaft, Hamburg
209.	*James Spier* [168]	1896 Nov 24	Schooner, steam-aux, 195' LOD, 34" beam, 15' draft	Benicia	Inter-island Navigation Co. Hawaii
210.	*La Chilena*	1897 May 24	Schooner, naphtha-aux, 10.70 tons, 41' LOD, 14' beam, 4.8' draft	Benicia	Campbell Company
211.	*Neptune*	1897 Dec	Schooner, 140 tons, 104' LOD, 24' beam, 7.1' draft	Benicia	A.G. Jaluit-Gesellschaft, Hamburg
212.	*Leah*	1897 Sept	Steamer, stern-wheel, 477 tons, 138.7' LOD, 31' beam, 6.3' draft, price $80,000	Benicia	Northern Commercial Co. St Michaels, Alaska
213.	*Pride of the Bay* [169]	1897 Mar 14	Sloop yacht, 40' LOD	Benicia	Matthew Turner
214.	*Villain* [170]	1897 Mar 25	Schooner, yacht	Benicia	Matthew Turner
215.	*Fox* [171]	1898	Schooner-rigged lighter, 539 tons	Benicia	Northern Commercial Co. St Michaels, Alaska
216.	*Bear* [172]	1898	Schooner-rigged lighter, 539 tons	Benicia	Northern Commercial Co. St Michaels, Alaska
217.	*Hercules*	1898 Jan	Schooner, steam-screw, 150 tons, 106' LOD, 25' beam, 10' draft	Benicia	A.G. Jaluit-Gesellschaft, Hamburg
218.	*Clara*	1898 June 11	Steamer, stern-wheel, 81.52 tons, 75.5' LOD, 22' beam, 4.6' draft	Benicia	California & Northwest Trading & Mining Company
219.	*Mary Sachs*	1898 Apr 22	Schooner, twin screw, two 30 HP engines, 35.31 tons, 56.5' LOD, 18.2' beam, 5.6' draft, price $5,000	Benicia	Lippman Sachs, Sachs Brothers and Company
220.	*Alice Rix*	1898 March	Steamer, stern-wheel, 100' LOD	Benicia	Union Shipping and Transportation Co.

221.	*Bessie H.*	1898 March	Steamer, stern-wheel, 175' LOD, Sub-assembled and shipped to Alaska	Benicia	Pacific Coast Commercial Co.
222.	*W. P. Fuller*	1898 June 30	Schooner, twin screw gas, 49.07 tons, 76,5' LOD, 18.5' beam, 5.3' draft	Benicia	W. P. Fuller & Company
223.	*Queen of the Isles*	1898 July	Schooner, kerosene-aux, 50 HP, 95' LOD, 24' beam, 9' draft	Benicia	Wilkins & Company
224.	*Malolo*	1898 July	Schooner, gas-screw, 29 tons, 60.8' LOD, 15.2' beam, 5.8' draft, price $7,000	Benicia	John Sass Hawaiian Registry
225.	*San Jose*	1898 Aug 19	Steamer, stern-wheel, 192.45 tons, 101' LOD, 28' beam, 5.8' draft	Benicia	Robert Christie
226.	*Mascotte*	1898 Nov 18	Schooner, 95" LOD, 34' beam, 9' draft	Benicia	Hernsheim & Co. of Hamburg
227.	*Monarch*	1898	Barge, lighter, 153 tons	Benicia	Dawson City, Yukon
228.	*Taku*	1898	Steamer, 54 tons	Benicia	Unknown
229.	*Marshalleon*	1899 Jan	Schooner, 40 tons, 63' LOD, 28' beam, 6' draft	Benicia	Jaluit Company of Hamburg
230.	*Alba*	1899 Jan	Schooner, 63' LOD, 18' beam, 6' draft	Benicia	Mexican owners
231.	*Ebon*	1899 Jan	Schooner, 63' LOD, 18' beam, 6' draft	Benicia	A.G. Jaluit-Gesellschaft, Hamburg
232.	*Caroline*	1899 Mar 9	Sloop. Gas-screw, 14.90 tons, 41.9' LOD, 16' beam, 3.2' draft	Benicia	SF freight business
233.	*Gadder*	1899 Sept 17	Sloop, yacht, 25.5' LOD, 8.5' beam	Benicia	Matthew Turner
234.	*Benicia*[173]	1899 Sept 23	Barkentine, 674 tons, 169' LOD, 40' beam, 14' draft	Benicia	Captain E. C. Bowes
235.	*Tamarii Tahiti*	1899 Nov 23	Schooner, 145 tons.	Benicia	Capt. George Dexter Tahiti trade French Registry
236.	*Surprise*	1899 Dec	Schooner, gas-aux, 147 tons, 95' LOD, 18.2' beam, 8.7' draft	Benicia	M. W. McChesney & Company of Hawaii
237.	*Catherine*	1899	Sloop, yacht, 60' LOD, 9.7' beam, 3.5' draft	Benicia	Archie Sutherland

238.	*Eclipse*	1900 March	Schooner, gas aux, 125 HP, 211 tons, 104' LOD, 27' beam, 10.2' draft	Benicia	R. N. McChesney Hawaiian Registry
239.	*Bonita*[174]	1900 Mar 27	Schooner, 14 tons	Benicia	George Genereaux
240.	*York*	1900 March	Schooner-rigged lighter, 231 tons, 131' LOD, 34' beam, 7' draft	Benicia	Alaska Commercial Company
241.	*Nome*	1900 March	Schooner-rigged lighter, 231 tons, 131' LOD, 34' beam, 7' draft	Benicia	Alaska Commercial Company
242.	*Rosamond*	1900 May 19	Schooner, 4-masted, 1,387 tons, 210' LOD, 41' beam, 17' draft	Benicia	Williams, Dimond and Company
243.	*Captain Blair*	1900 May	Schooner, 130' LOD, 32' beam, 10' draft	Benicia	Alaska Commercial Company
244.	*Aeolus*	1900 July	Schooner, gas aux. 150 tons, 104.9' LOD, 24" beam, 9.6" draft	Benicia	A.G. Jaluit-Gesellschaft, Hamburg
245.	*Ariel*	1900 Aug 30	Schooner, 4-masted, 726 tons, 176' LOD, 40' beam, 14.5' draft	Benicia	U. Andrews San Francisco
246.	*Pathfinder*	1900 Nov 10	Schooner, pilot, 86 tons, 81' LOD, 24' beam, 14.5' draft	Benicia	San Francisco Bar Pilots
247.	*La Croix du Sud*	1900 Dec	Schooner, 45 tons, 63' LOD, 18' beam, 6' draft	Benicia	Tahiti owners
248.	*The Crowley*	1900	Schooner, gas-aux	Benicia	The Crowley Brothers
249.	*Maurice*	1901 Jan 12	Schooner, 63' LOD, 18' beam, 6' draft	Benicia	Tahiti owners
250.	*Nuku Hiva*	1901 Jan	Schooner, 50 tons, 65' LOD, 18' beam, 6' draft	Benicia	Société Comm. de l'Océanie, Hamburg
251.	*Solano*	1901 Mar 1	Schooner, 4-masted, 728 tons, 175' LOD, 40' beam, 14.5' draft	Benicia	Alaska Salmon Packing Company
252.	*Jilt*[175]	1901 May	Sloop, yacht, 67' LOD, 22" beam, 6' draft	Benicia	F. J. Croall San Francisco Yacht Club
253.	*Helen*[176]	1901 June 2	Sloop, yacht, 32' LOD, 11' beam, 4.5' draft	Benicia	A. E Chapman San Francisco
254.	*Amaranth*	1901 July 22	Barkentine, 4-masted, 1,109 tons, 209' LOD, 42.5' beam, 18' draft	Benicia	Nelson Andrews San Francisco
255.	*Newtown*	1901	Steamer, stern-wheel, 77 tons, 75' LOD, 20' beam, 5' draft	Benicia	O. Johnson San Francisco

256.	*Amazon*	1902 Feb 1	Barkentine, 4-masted, 1,167 tons, 209' LOD, 42.5' beam, 19' draft	Benicia	Nelson Andrews San Francisco
257.	*Gazelle*	1902 Feb	Schooner, gas-aux, 112' LOD, 30' beam, 12' draft	Benicia	Hersheim & Co. Matupi, Hamburg
258.	*Matthew Turner*	1902 June 28	Schooner, 4-masted, 816 tons, 182' LOD, 42.2' beam, 15' draft	Benicia	Matthew Turner
259.	*Eimeo*	1902 July 7	Schooner, gas aux, 175 tons, 106' LOD, 24' beam, 10' draft	Benicia	Société Comm. de l'Océanie, Hamburg
260.	*Tarang*	1902 Nov	Schooner, gas screw, 83 tons, 69.5' LOD, 22.2' beam, 8' draft	Benicia	Papua New Guinea
261.	*Hope*	1902	Barge, 120 feet long, 400 tons, 37' beam, 9' draft	Benicia	Newtown Trans. Co. Port Costa to Sacramento Fleet
262.	*Triton*	1903 Jan	Schooner, gas screw, 150 tons, 75 HP, 107' LOD, 24' beam, 10' draft	Benicia	A.G. Jaluit-Gesellschaft, Hamburg
263.	*Siafiafi*	1903 Feb	Schooner, 38.77 tons, 60.5' LOD, 18' beam, 6' draft	Benicia	French Polynesia
264.	*Catherina*[177]	1903 Aug	Barge, 140' LOD, 32' beam, 6' draft	Benicia	Newtown Trans. Co., Port Costa to Sacramento Fleet
265.	*St. Michael*[178]	1904 October	Schooner, gas auxiliary, 60 HP, 85' LOD, 25' beam, 7' draft	Benicia	Marché Colonial Company, Paris

Summary of the 265 Vessel Types Built:

| 173 | Schooners | 4 | Barkentines | 3 | Brigantines |
| 28 | Yacht | 21 | Steamers | 13 | Half-brigantines |

Part of the vessel research is compounded by the use of repetitive names for some of Matthew Turner's ships. Here is a list of the repetitive names:

Alert, 1883 steam tug built in San Francisco, sold to John D. Spreckels.
Alert, 1885 steam tug built in Benicia, sold to John D. Spreckels.

Alice, 1888 stern wheel steamer built in Benicia for Pacific Pac & Nav.
Alice, 1895 stern wheel steamer built in Benicia for Pacific Pac & Nav.

Bella, 1876 schooner built in San Francisco, sold to Alaska Commercial Company.
Bella, 1886 stern-wheel schooner built in Benicia, sold to Northern Commercial Co.

Benicia, 1891 schooner scow built in Benicia, sold to Albert Eriksen, SF.
Benicia, 1899 brigantine built in Benicia, sold to Captain E. C. Bowes.

Consuelo, 1877 schooner yacht built in San Francisco, sold to Commodore Isadore Gutte.
Consuelo, 1880 half brigantine built in San Francisco, sold to John D, Spreckels.

Emma, 1885 2-masted schooner, built in Benicia, sold to Mexican owners.
Emma, 1890 2-masted schooner, built in Benicia, sold to Captain Brown Benson, Alaska.

Eva, 1882 2-masted schooner, built in San Francisco, sold to J. Kentfield & Company.
Eva, 1889 2-masted schooner, built in Benicia.

Kodiak, 1881 schooner, built in San Francisco, sold to Alaska Commercial Company.
Kodiak, 1895 schooner, built in Benicia, sold to Alaska Commercial Company.

Lurline, 1883 schooner yacht, built in San Francisco, sold to J.D. Spreckels.
Lurline, 1887 half-brigantine, built in Benicia, sold to J.D. Spreckels.

Marion, 1872, schooner, built in San Francisco, sold to Tahiti.
Marion, 1882, 2-masted schooner, built in San Francisco, sold to Oliver Smith & Co. SF.

Matthew Turner, 1877 schooner, built in San Francisco, sold to Commodore Isadore Gutte.
Matthew Turner, 1902 4-masted schooner, built in Benicia, for Matthew Turner.

Nellie, 1879 sloop yacht, built in San Francisco, sold to Hyde R. Bowie, San Francisco.
Nellie, 1880 sloop yacht, built in San Francisco, sold to Hyde R. Bowie, San Francisco.
Nellie, 1884 schooner yacht, built in Benicia, sold to Peter J. Donahue. San Francisco.
Nellie, 1887 schooner yacht built in Benicia, sold to J. Mervyn Donahue, San Francisco

Nuku Hiva, 1881, 2-masted schooner, built in San Francisco, sold to the French Government.
Nuku Hiva, 1900, 2-masted schooner, built in Benicia, sold to Société Com. de l'Océanie, Hamburg.

Papeete, 1883, 2-masted schooner, built in San Francisco, sold to the Turner & Chapman Company.
Papeete, 1892, 2-masted schooner, built in Benicia, sold to the French Government for a gunboat.

Pearl, 1876, 2-mastedschooner yacht, built in San Francisco, sold to Commodore John Eckley.
Pearl, 1886, 2-masted schooner, built in Benicia, sold to Louis Sloss, San Francisco.
Reliance, 1886 2-masted schooner, built in Benicia, sold to Louis Sloss, San Francisco.
Reliance, 1889 steam screw schooner, built in Benicia, sold to John D. Spreckels, San Francisco.

San Jose, 1886, 2-matred schooner, built in Benicia, sold to James Girvan, San Francisco.
San Jose, 1898, stern wheel schooner, built in Benicia, sold to Robert Christie.

Solano, 1895, scow schooner, built in Benicia, sold to Piper, Aden, & Goodall Company.
Solano, 1901, 4-masted schooner, built in Benicia, sold to the Alaska Packing Company.

St. Paul, 1879, steamer, built in San Francisco, sold to the Alaska Commercial Company.

St. Paul, 1890, 2-masted schooner, built in Benicia, sold to M. L. Washburne, Kodiak, Alaska.

APPENDIX B
Sailing Records of Matthew Turner Ships

The following is a listing of fast passages by Turner-built vessels, listed in order of year built.

Nautilus 1868 brigantine: San Francisco to Tahiti, 17 days
Tahiti to San Francisco, 19 days.

John D, Spreckels 1880 brigantine: Round trip San Francisco to Kahului, 28 days.

W. H. Dimond 1881 barkentine: Honolulu to San Francisco, 9 days, 10 hours

Anna 1881 schooner: Honolulu to San Francisco, 10 days in 1886.

William G. Erwin 1881 brigantine: San Francisco to Kahului, 8 days, 17 hours
Honolulu to San Francisco, 9 days.

Emma Claudina 1882 3-mast schooner: San Francisco to Hawaii, 8 days, 8 hours.

Lurline 1883 yacht, won three of the first four San Pedro to Diamond Head, Honolulu yacht races, the Transpacific Yacht Race (TransPac).

Galilee 1891 brigantine: Tahiti to San Francisco, 22 ½ days, averaged 28 ½ days in 21 consecutive trips.

Geneva	1892 brigantine: Launceton, Tasmania to Newcastle NSW 2 days.
Benicia	1899 barkentine: Newcastle NSW to Kehel, Hawaii, 35 days.
Solano	1901 4-mast schooner: Shanghai to Port Townsend, Washington, 22 ½ days in 1902.
Amaranth	1901 4-mast schooner: Shanghai to Astoria, Oregon, 13 days.

APPENDIX C
Known Fates of Matthew Turner Ships[179]

Amaranth	1901 4-mast barkentine	Wrecked at Jarvis Island, AK 1913.
Amazon	1902 4-mast barkentine	Burned at sea July 4, 1925.
Amethyst	1883 2-masted schooner	Wrecked in storm, Coquille, OR, Mar 1902
Anna	1881 2-masted schooner	Wrecked in Bering Sea 1902.
Arctic	1889 Stern wheel schooner	Wrecked on reef at Yukon River, Oct 1889.
Ariel	1900 4-masted schooner	Wrecked Inuboyesaki, Japan 1917.
Bella	1888 schooner	Lost on Unimak Island, AK, February 1899.
Benicia	1899 3-masted barkentine	Wrecked on Lafolle Reef, Haiti, Oct 10, 1920.
Bertha	1888 steam brigantine	Wrecked on Harold Island, AK Feb 1902.
Berwick	1887 2-masted schooner	Wrecked at Siuslaw, OR Mar 13, 1908.
Canute	1882 2-masted schooner	Abandon in Honolulu in 1927.

Chetco	1887 2-masted schooner	Burned at Summerland, CA Fed 19, 1918.
Cometa	1883 2-masted schooner	Wrecked by a storm near Altata, MX Oct 1896.
Courtney Ford	1883 brigantine	Wrecked Glen Island, AK Sept 7, 1902.
Czar	1881 2-masted schooner	Sold to Mexico 1920, renamed Juan Lanzagorta
Dagmar	1877 schooner	Lost on trip from Petropavlovsk, Jan 1878
Del Norte	1887 2-masted schooner	Lost near Punta Gorda, CA, 1906
Eimeo	1902 schooner, gas aux.	Wrecked on reef of Tuamotu Islands Sept 1904
Emma Claudina	1882 3-masted schooner	Sunk off Grays Harbor Nov 14, 1906
Equator	1888 2-masted schooner	Wrecked at Quillayute Bar, WA, Oct 23, 1923
Ester Cobos	1878 schooner	Wrecked on Rouge River, OR, Oct 21, 1879
Eureka	1887 2-masted schooner	Wrecked on Coquille River bar, Nov 30, 1889
Galilee	1891 brigantine	Bow at Museum of History Benicia, Stern at Fort Mason, San Francisco.

Garcia	1882 2-masted schooner	Wrecked near Cape Mearnes, OR, Dec 12, 1893
Geneva	1892 brigantine	Burned in Gulf of Mexico June 11, 1926.
Gracie B. Richardson	1885 2-masted schooner	Aground at Fisk's Mill Cove, CA Dec 1888
Herman	1890 2-masted schooner	Sold to Tahiti owners, renamed Roberta 1930.
Hope	1902 barge	Wrecked on the Feather River February 1909.
J. C. Ford	1882 3-masted schooner	Wrecked at Grays Harbor, WA, Feb 17, 1893.
John D. Spreckels	1880 brigantine	Wrecked off Pt. Reyes, CA, March 29, 1913.
Joseph & Henry	1892 2-masted schooner	Wrecked off cape Mendocino December 1900.
Karluk	1884 brigantine steamer	Crushed and sank in Arctic ice January 1914.
Kodiak	1881 2-masted schooner	Wrecked in Alaska on April 14, 1895.
Leah	1897 stern-wheel steamer	Wrecked on Yukon River September 1906
Lizzie Merrill	1885 2-masted schooner	Wrecked in reefs at Whitesboro, CA Dec 1994.
Lurline	1887 brigantine	Sunk in collision off Santa Cruz, Jan 15, 1915.

M. Romero Rubio	1886 auxiliary schooner	Wrecked ashore, Coronado Beach, Aug 1886.
Malolo	1898 schooner	Wrecked in storm, Clayoquot Sound, Dec 1920.
Mascotte	1898 auxiliary schooner	Caught fire and burnt at Bougainville Is, July 1901.
Mary Sachs	1898 schooner	Wrecked on Banks Island, Canada, August, 1917.
Matthew Turner	1877 schooner	Destroyed in hurricane off Japan May 1894.
Marion	1882 2-masted schooner	Wrecked Sanak Island, AK, April 11, 1906.
Nautilus	1868 brigantine	Wrecked in August 1895, Hereheretue Island
Navigator	1885 schooner	Capsized in heavy seas off Samoan Is. Jan 1886
Newark	1887 2-masted schooner	Remains in mud at San Pedro Harbor, 1930.
Nome	1900 2-masted schooner	Lost in Alaska, 1901.
Portia	1888 2-masted schooner	Wrecked at Stewart's Point, CA October 1899.
Pitcairn	1890 2-masted schooner	Wrecked in Mindoro, PI, Oct 17, 1912.
Rosamond	1900 4-masted schooner	Laid up Lake Union, Seattle, WA, 1928.

Rosario	1878 3-masted schooner	Crushed in ice serving as whaler, July 2, 1898.
St. George	1878 2-masted schooner	Wrecked St. Paul Harbor, AK, April 27, 1881.
Santa Cruz	1893 2-masted schooner	Sunk in storm at Santa Cruz Is, Dec 1960.
Selina	1883 brigantine	Wrecked entering Hilo Harbor, HI 1887.
Seven Sisters	1888 2-masted schooner	Lost Cape Espenberg, AK, Sept 1, 1908.
Solano	1901 4-masted schooner	Wrecked near Ocean Park, WA, Feb 5, 1907.
Tahiti	1881 brigantine	Capsized off Mexican coast, September 1891.
Tamaru Tahiti	1889 2-masted schooner	Capsized and sank at Tahiti June 8, 1966.
Theodore H. Allen	1875 pilot schooner	Collision off California coast January 1888.
Vesta	1882 3-masted schooner	Wrecked near Nitinat, BC Dec 10, 1897.
W. H. Dimond	1881 barkentine	Lost on Bird Island, AK, Feb 10, 1914.
William G. Erwin	1881 brigantine	Burned for movie Catalina Is., CA May 1926.
York	1900 2-masted schooner	Lost the same year in Alaska.

APPENDIX D
Ship Types of the 19th Century

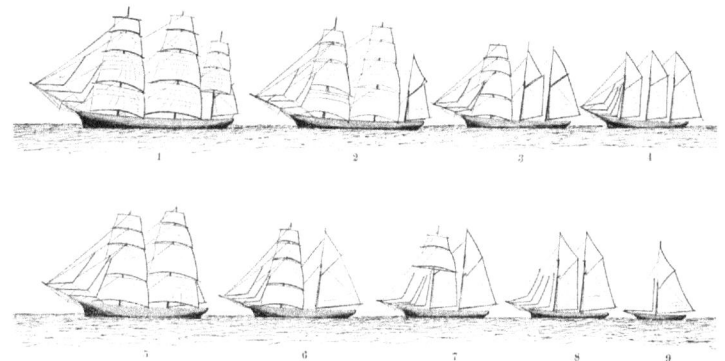

1. Full-rigged ship: at least three masts, fully square-rigged.
2. Barque: three to five masts with a fore-and-aft rigged mizzen mast.
3. Barkentine: three masts, only the foremast is square-rigged.
4. Three-mast schooner: three masts, fully fore-and-aft rigged.
5. Brig and brigantine: Both rigs are two-masted vessels with mainmast and foremast.

    A brig is a two masted sailing craft, square rigged on both masts; a brigantine is a two masted sailing ship rigged with square sails on the foremast and fore and aft sails, typically gaff rigged on the aft or main mast. Historically the masts on a brig would be made in three sections, main mast, main top mast and main topgallant and the same for the foremast, whereas a brigantine has masts only made in two sections.

6. Half-brigantine, schooner brig: two masts, with a square-rigged foremast and a fore-and-aft rigged main mast. This half brig-half schooner requires less crew to operate.
7. Topsail schooner: at least two masts, at least one of them with a square-rigged masthead.
8. Two-mast schooner: two masts, fully fore-and-aft rigged.
9. Sloop: one mast with a main and a head sail.

Appendix E
Glossary of Nautical Terminology

Aft: Aft is the inside (on board) rearmost part of the vessel.

Aloft: The higher masthead or the higher rigging.

Barkentine: A barque, barc, or bark is a type of sailing vessel with three or more masts and mainmasts rigged square and only the mizzen rigged fore and aft.

Billet Head: The billet head is a decorative piece of woodwork that adorns the bow of a ship.

Binnacle: A waist-high stand on the deck of a ship mounted in front of the helmsman, containing navigational instruments.

Boom: This pole runs perpendicular to the mast and holds the bottom of the mainsail in place.

Bowsprit: A large pole sticking out from the bow of a ship, used as securing points for lines attached to the forward sails.

Brigantine: In modern American terminology, the term brigantine usually means a vessel with the foremast square-rigged and the mainmast fore-and-aft rigged without any square sails.

Brig: A brig has been used in the past as an abbreviation of brigantine. The brig developed as a variant of the brigantine. Re-rigging a brigantine with two square-rigged masts instead of one gave it greater sailing power and required fewer men or 'hands' to work them.

Bulwark: An extension of a ship's sides above the level of the deck.

Cathead: A large wooden beam located on either bow of a sailing ship, and angled outward at roughly 45 degrees. The beam is used to support the ship's anchor when raising or lowering it

Clipper: A clipper is a sailing vessel designed for speed, a priority that takes precedence over cargo-carrying capacity or building or operating costs. It is not restricted to any one rig.

Dinghy: A small boat that is used to travel to shore from the main vessel.

Donkey lighter: A barge with a steam powered wench.

Ferris design: A ship designed by Theodore Ferris, was a wood-hulled cargo ship design approved for production by the United States Shipping Board's Emergency Fleet Corporation.

Gaff: A free-swinging spar attached to the top of a sail.

Half-brigantine: A square-rigged brig only on the foremast. Also known as a hermaphrodite brig.

Jib: A triangular foresail in front of the foremast.

Jib-boom: A spar used to extend the length of a bowsprit on sailing ships

Keel: The keel is a specific part of the hull. It is the main beam that runs from the front (bow) of the boat to the back (stern) and goes through the middle of the vessel.

Lazarette: A small compartment below the deck in the after end of a vessel, used for stores.

Leeward: In the direction that the wind is blowing towards.

Lighter: A shallow-drafted vessel used to load and unload ships not docked at piers.

Mast ladder: A rope ladder extending from the deck of a ship to the mast.

Metaled or metallized: The use of copper plates affixed to the surface of the hull below the waterline, for protecting a wooden vessel from attack by shipworms, barnacles, and other marine growth.

Mizzen: The name of the third, aftermost mast of a square-rigged ship or a three masted schooner.

Mold loft: A large building with a floor where the lines of a ship are laid down full size and molds and templates made from them.

Oakum: Oakum was a key fibrous component in the caulking process to waterproof ships (fibrous rope mixed with pine tar).

Packet line: In the 19th Century the term meant a schooner or steamer line operating on a regular, fixed daily schedule between two or more cities. Usually, it carried packets of mail, government mail contracts, passengers, and cargo such as lumber or fruit.

Pilot schooner: Small schooners used for guiding arriving vessels to safe anchorage at their port.

Port: Port is always the left-hand side of the boat when you are facing the bow.

Rigging: The system of masts and lines on ships and other sailing vessels.

Schooner: A sailing ship rigged with fore-and-aft sails on its two or more masts.

Scow: A large flat-bottomed boat with broad, square ends used along coastal trade routes for transporting bulk materials.

Screw: A boat's propeller.

Ship's bell: Striking the ship's bell is the traditional method of marking time and regulating the crew's watches.

Side-wheel schooner: Powered with a paddlewheel on the side.

Sloop: A single-masted sailing vessel with fore-and-aft rigging, including mainsail.

Spar: A term used for any wood or metal pole, such as mast or boom, used to give shape to sails.

Starboard: Starboard is always the right-hand side of the boat when you are facing the bow.

Stays: Stays are ropes, wires, or rods on sailing vessels that run fore-and-aft along the centerline from the masts to the hull, deck, bowsprit, or to other masts which serve to stabilize the masts.

Stern: Stern refers to the outside rearmost part of the vessel.

Stern-wheel schooner: Powered with a paddlewheel on the stern.

Stun'sail: An extra sail on a square-rigged vessel for use in fair weather for extra speed.

Tender: A small boat that's used to transport passengers between their cruise ship and the port when the ship itself is unable to dock.

Way: A structure that supports the ship under construction, usually at the waterline.

Williwaw: The williwaw is a wind resulting from the descent of cold, dense air from coastal mountains in high latitudes. When it reaches the bottom of the mountain, the wind blows along the coastline and out to sea producing powerful gusts.

Windjammer: A commercial sailing ship with multiple masts that may be square-rigged, fore-and-aft rigged, or a combination of the two. The informal term "windjammer" arose during the transition from the Age of Sail to the Age of Steam during the 19th Century.

Windlass: A machine used on ships that is used to let-out and raise-up equipment such as a ship's anchor.

Windward: The direction in which the wind is currently blowing.

Whaleback: A whaleback was a type of cargo steamship of unusual design, with a hull that continuously curved above the waterline from vertical to horizontal.

Yawl: A two-masted fore-and-aft-rigged sailboat with the mizzen mast stepped far aft so that the mizzen boom overhangs the stern.

Works Cited

1. Upton, Harriett Taylor, *History of the Western Reserve,* Lewis Publishing Co., 1910, page 1474.
2. Marks, Ben, *Wind Power: How the 19th-Century's Greatest Shipbuilder Opened the Pacific,* 2019.
3. *Geneva Times, Ship-Building,* January 24, 1878.
4. Feather, Carl E., *Success Born of Grief, Star Beacon,* Dec 10, 2011.
5. *Indian Creek and shipbuilding industry,* Geneva-on-the-Lake Heritage Trail website.
6. Ibid.
7. Ibid.
8. Ibid.
9. *Emily Atkins Turner,* Ancestry.com.
10. Oliver, Don. K., *Full Many a Gallant Ship,* page 24, San Francisco Maritime National Historical Library.
11. Feather, Carl E., *Success Born of Grief, Star Beacon,* Dec 10, 2011.
12. *Indian Creek and shipbuilding industry,* Geneva-on-the-Lake Heritage Trail website.
13. Bliss, Alice, *The Jefferson Gazette, 'Round About,* April 30, 1973.
14. Feather, Carl E., *Success Born of Grief, Star Beacon* Dec 10, 2011.
15. *The Gerald C. Metzler, Great Vessel Lakes Database, G. R. Roberts* (Schooner, 1848), Wisconsin Maritime Museum.
16. *The Early Years: Biographical Information on Matthew Turner, Chapter 1850c,* San Francisco Maritime National Historical Library.
17. Bliss, Alice, *The Jefferson Gazette, 'Round About,* April 30, 1973.
18. Ibid.
19. *The Early Years: Biographical Information on Matthew Turner, Chapter 1849-1850,* San Francisco Maritime National Historical Library.
20. *Daily Alta California,* August 25, 1851, *Vessels Advertised.* page 3
21. Ashtabula County Genealogical Society, Inc.
22. Bliss, Alice, *The Jefferson Gazette, 'Round About,* April 30, 1973.
23. *Daily Pacific News,* May 2, 1850, *Marine News, Port of San Francisco, Arrived,* page 2.
24. *Matthew Turner Chronology, Chapter 1854b,* San Francisco Maritime National Historical Library.

25   Marks, Ben, *Wind Power: How the 19th-Century's Greatest Shipbuilder Opened the Pacific*, 2019.
26   Oliver, Don. K., *Full Many a Gallant Ship*, Chapter 1853-1854, San Francisco Maritime National Historical Library.
27   Praetzellis, Mary, M.A., Praetzellis, Adrian, Ph. D., *South of Market: Historical Archaeology of 3 San Francisco Neighborhoods,* 2009, page 70.
28   Oliver, Don. K., *Full Many a Gallant Ship*, Chapter 1853-1854, San Francisco Maritime National Historical Library.
29   Ibid.
30   Feather, Carl E., *Success Born of Grief, Star Beacon,* Dec 10, 2011.
31   Oliver, Don. K., *Full Many a Gallant Ship*, Chapter 1853-1854, San Francisco Maritime National Historical Library.
32   Ibid.
33   Ibid.
34   Oliver, Don. K., *Full Many a Gallant Ship*, Chapter 1855, San Francisco Maritime National Historical Library.
35   Hunt, Murray C., *Captain Matthew Turner*, self-published.
36   Oliver, Don. K., *Full Many a Gallant Ship*, Chapter 1856, San Francisco Maritime National Historical Library.
37   Wilcox, W. A., Field Agent, *Interview with Matthew Turner*, United States Bureau of Fisheries, 1888.
38   Oliver, Don. K., *Full Many a Gallant Ship*, Chapter 1857, San Francisco Maritime National Historical Library.
39   *Yanks in the Redwoods: Carving Out a Life in Northern California.*
40   *Summary of Years,* Matthew Turner Foundation, 1994.
41   Lyman, John, *An Old California Shipbuilder,* Cornell Maritime Press, 1942.
42   Ibid.
43   Ibid.
44   Ibid.
45   *Sacramento Daily Union,* October 17, 1866, *More Codfish*, page 2.
46   Oliver, Don K., *Nautilus: First of Many*, Matthew Turner Foundation, 1990.
47   Ibid.
48   Ibid.
49   Ibid.
50   Ibid.
51   Ibid.

52 Lynch, Tim, *The Historical Place of Matthew Turner*, 2012.
53 Oliver, Don K., *Maritime Heritage, The Biography of Matthew Turner*, 1965.
54 Kelly, Roger E. and Franklin, Gary, *Along the Shores of Time: Submerged Historic & Indigenous Resources in The Pacific Rim Region*, Proceedings from an International and Interdisciplinary Conference, March 31-April 3, 1999.
55 Ibid.
56 *Summary of Years*, Matthew Turner Foundation, 1994.
57 *Matthew Turner Research Notes*, Volume 6, HDC1702, San Francisco Maritime National Historical Library.
58 Ibid.
59 Hunt, Murray C., *Captain Matthew Turner*, self-published, 2008.
60 Karting, Herbert, *Schiffbaumeister Matthew Turner*, 2010, page 76-78.
61 *Daily Alta California*, February 14, 1874, *Ship Models for Japan*, page 1.
62 *San Francisco Call*, November 28, 1898, *The Wreck of the Rosario*, page 10.
63 *San Francisco Call*, August 19, 1894, *Sam Clarks Coin*, page 17.
64 Hosley, C. Thomas, *Eva's Childhood Recollections of the Matthew Turner Shipyard, Solano Historian*, May 1993.
65 Ibid.
66 Ibid.
67 Ibid.
68 Ibid.
69 Ibid.
70 *Sacramento Daily Union*, October 2, 1885, *A Benicia Lodging House Burned*, page 1.
71 *San Francisco Chronicle*, August 14, 1883, *Sportsman's Niche*, page 3.
72 *Daily Alta California, Afloat and Ashore*, March 3, 1888, page 2.
73 *Matthew Turner Ship Documentation, Poor Beggar*, San Francisco Maritime National Historical Library.
74 *The Geneva Times*, July 25, 1882.
75 Feather, Carl E., *Success Born of Grief, Star Beacon*, Dec 10, 2011.
76 *Los Angeles Herald*, December 26, 1896, *The First Whaleback*, page 1.
77 National Register of Historic Places, Whaling Bark *Stamboul*, 1988.
78 Ibid.
79 *San Francisco Morning Call*, March 1, 1895, *Benicia's Big Drydock*, page 1.
80 Badger, Margaret and Clinton, Larry, *The Story of the Galilee*, Sausalito Historical Society, 2020.
81 Note: The brigantine *Nautilus* holds the actual record; San Francisco to

Tahiti (17 days) and Tahiti to San Francisco return (19 days) in 1868.

82 Wikipedia, *Galilee* (ship).
83 Ibid.
84 Ibid.
85 Hunt, Murray C., *Captain Matthew Turner*, self-published, 2008
86 Lyman, John, *An Old California Shipbuilder*, Cornell Maritime Press, 1942.
87 Hunt, Murray C., *Captain Matthew Turner*, self-published, 2008.
88 Hosley, C. Thomas, *Eva's Childhood Recollections of the Matthew Turner Shipyard, Solano Historian*, May 1993.
89 *San Francisco Call*, August 7, 1902, *Will Go to Australia*, page 12.
90 *The Solano-Napa News Chronicle*, July 15, 1901, page 3.
91 *Pacific Rural Press,* August 31, 1901, *Farmers' Steamboat on the " Sacramento*, page 142.
92 Hosley, C. Thomas, *Eva's Childhood Recollections of the Matthew Turner Shipyard, Solano Historian*, May 1993.
93 Ibid.
94 Ibid.
95 Ibid.
96 Ibid.
97 Ibid.
98 Feather, Carl E., *Success Born of Grief, Star Beacon* Dec 10, 2011.
99 Hunt, Murray C., *Captain Matthew Turner*, self-published, 2008.
100 Lynch, Tim, *The Historical Place of Matthew Turner*, 2012.
101 *Humboldt Times*, September 2, 1906, *The Hoquiam is Launched*, page 8.
102 Hunt, Murray, *Captain Matthew Turner*, self-published, 2008.
103 Ibid.
104 National Register of Historic Places, Matthew Turner/James Robertson Shipyard, 1986.
105 Ibid.
106 *The Ark Sausalito: S.S. Charles Van Damme Ferry*, OurSausalito.com.
107 National Register of Historic Places, Matthew Turner/James Robertson Shipyard, 1986.
108 Tahaj, Katy, *The Fiery Story of the Schooner J. C. Ford*, 2019.
109 Matson Navigation Company website, *History.*
110 Hector, Bruce and Marzolla, A. Michael, *The Story of the Schooner Santa Cruz*, 2009.
111 *Robert Louis Stevenson and the Cruise on the Equator*, RLS website.

112 *San Francisco Examiner*, March 31, 1897, *Two Other Collisions*, page 14.

113 *Oakland Enquirer*, February 6, 1899, *An Important Business Established on the Estuary*, page 3.

114 Mielke, Coleen, *The History of the SS Dora*, 2023.

115 John Lyman, *Pacific Coast Built Sailers 1850-1905*, *The Marine Digest*, 1941.

116 Wikipedia, *Pitcairn* (schooner).

117 Vataja, Roy, *Aberdeen 1899: The embattled Benicia*, October 7, 2017.

118 *San Francisco Call*, December 19, 1912, *Madman Kills Self and Mate*, page 3.

119 Antoni, Judit, *In Search of Adventure: Count Rudolf Festetics and the Tolna's Journeys in the Pacific, Tribal Arts Magazine,* March 2020.

120 *San Francisco Call,* December 28, 1900, *Count Rudolph Charges Under Oath that Countess Elia Festetics de Tolna is a Flirt*, page 1.

121 *Los Angeles Herald*, November 15, 1900, *Cannibal Islanders of the South Seas*, page 1.

122 Oliver, Don K., *Pilot Schooner America*, Matthew Turner Foundation, 1990.

123 Pennelope Goforth, *Dastardly Deed Strands Schooner Courtney Ford, The Sea Chest,* September 2015.

124 *San Francisco Call,* December 5, 1890, *Last Trip in the Line*, page 6.

125 *Los Angeles Herald,* November 30, 1891, *A Slave Ship's Fate*, page 1.

126 *Vestkusten,* December 11, 1891, page 4.

127 *San Francisco Examiner*, November 30, 1891, *In Unwanted Garb*, page 3.

128 *San Luis Obispo Morning Tribune*, April 27, 1892, *The Lost Tahiti*, page 1.

129 *Los Angeles Herald,* July 21, 1892, *Hardships on the High Seas*, page 4.

130 *San Francisco Examiner*, November 30, 1891, *Schooner Well Known Here*, page 3.

131 *Marin County Tocsin,* August 27, 1898, *County News*, page 3.

132 *San Francisco Call*, September 21, 1908, *Yachtmen Cruise Out Beyond the Heads*, page 9.

133 *Sausalito News*, October 16, 1936, *Twenty Years Ago*, page 7.

134 Kaffer, Dave Kaffer, *The Original "Salmon Capital of the World,"* SitNews, 2018.

135 Niven, Jennifer, *The Ice Master, The Doomed 1913 Voyage of the Karluk*, Hyperion, New York, 2000.

136 Heller, Avra, Project Manager, *The Brigantine Matthew Turner: The Bay*

Area's Educational Tall Ship, September 2017.
137   OurSausilito,com, Educational Sausalito Tall Ship - The *Matthew Turner*.
138   Matthew Turner Foundation, *1994 Matthew Turner Ship List*, 10th revision.
139   Ibid.
140   Ibid.
141   Ibid.
142   Ibid.
143   *Matthew Turner Research Notes*, Volume 6, San Francisco Maritime National Historical Library.
144   *Daily Alta California,* March 24, 1875, *Along the Wharves*, page 1.
145   *Daily Alta California,* August 28, 1876, *The New Yacht "Lalla Rookh,"* page 1.
146   *Daily Alta California,* July 24, 1876, *Along the Wharves*, page 2.
147   *Daily Alta California,* October 21, 1877 *A Review of Our Shipwrights' Labors*, page 1
148   *Daily Alta California,* February 2, 1879, *Along the Wharves*, page 2.
149   *Daily Alta California,* October 5, 1880, *Launch of the Schooner Yacht "Nellie,"* page 1.
150   Hunt, Murray C., *Captain Matthew Turner*, self-published, 2008.
151   *Daily Alta California,* April 25, 1884, *Along the Wharves*, page 1.
152   *The Daily San Diegan,* August 24, 1885, *Arrival of the Celia*, page 3.
153   *Sacramento Daily Union,* September 25, 1884, *Brief Notes*, page 3.
154   *Sacramento Daily Union,* January 21, 1885, *Tug Launches – Hazardous Navigation*, page 4.
155   *The Sausalito News,* March 25, 1885, *Yachting*, page 3.
156   *Daily Alta California,* May 7, 1885, *Along the Wharves*, page 7.
157   *Daily Alta California,* July 29, 1886, *Along the Wharves*, page 7.
158   *Los Angeles Herald,* December 26, 1896, *The First Whaleback*, page 1.
159   *Santa Cruz Sentinel,* April 1, 1887, *The Yachtsmen*, page 3.
160   Lyman, John, *Marine Digest, Pacific Coast-Built Sailers, 1850-1905,* February 15, 1941, page 2.
161   *Sausalito News,* August 15, 1890, *Sausalito Yachting News*, page 2.
162   *Daily Alta California,* September 4, 1890, *Afloat and Ashore*, page 6.
163   *San Francisco Call,* May 28, 1893, *They Skim the Salt Sea Wave*, page 1.
164   *San Francisco Call,* July 15, 1893, *Yachtings Jottings*, page 10
165   *San Francisco Call,* August 21, 1894, *A Strange Yarn*, page 6.

166 *San Francisco Call,* May 23, 1895, *The Schooner Came Back,* page 7.
167 Ibid
168 *San Francisco Call,* November 25, 1896, *A New Sreamer for Hawaii's Isle,* page 7.
169 *San Francisco Call.* March 20, 1897, *The Yachtsman,* page 8.
170 Ibid
171 Karting, Herbert, *Schiffbaumeister Matthew Turner,* 2010, page 38.
172 Ibid.
173 *San Francisco Call,* September 23, 1899, *Chapter of Accidents,* page 5.
174 *The San Francisco Call and Post,* April 1, 1900, *Yachtsmen Preparing for Season's Opening,* page 24.
175 *San Francisco Call,* May 25, 1901, *Big Regattas are on the Schedule,* page 10.
176 *San Francisco Call,* July 6, 1901, *Tiberon Tars Choose the Presto,* page 4.
177 *Benicia Herald,* August, 28, 1903.
178 *San Francisco Call,* October 25, 1904, "New Schooner St. Michael", page 7.
179 Gibbs, Jim, *Windjammers of the Pacific Rim,* Schiffer Publishing Ltd., 1987 (with updates by the author).
180 Luce, Stephen B., *Text-book of Seamanship: The Equipping and Handling of Vessels Under Sail or Steam; for the Use of the United States Naval Academy.* New York: Van Nostrand Co., 1891. Plate 4

About the Author

Author Allan Gandy

Allan Gandy is a California Polytechnic State University graduate, San Luis Obispo, with a degree in Metallurgical Engineering. He has been a resident of Benicia, California for over 45 years and has an interest in its history. He has previously written *The Sandstone Magazine at the Benicia Arsenal: Benicia's Little-known Gem*, *The Clock Tower: A History of Benicia's Mighty Fortress*, and *Images of America: The Benicia Arsenal*.

Allan is an amateur geologist who has a passion for studying the geology of California and volcanology. Additionally, he is interested in the California Gold Rush and has experience in prospecting for gold. Having lived in California for most of his life, he has a deep appreciation for the state's natural beauty, including the California coast, the redwood forests, the Shasta and Lassen volcanic landscapes, the Sierras, and other historic areas throughout the state. Allan is proud to live in Benicia where Mathew Turner produced 184 vessels in his shipyard and sailed the waters of the Carquinez Strait.

ABOOKS

ALIVE Book Publishing and ALIVE Publishing Group
are imprints of Advanced Publishing LLC,
3200 A Danville Blvd., Suite 204, Alamo, California 94507

Telephone: 925.837.7303
alivebookpublishing.com

www.ingramcontent.com/pod-product-compliance
Lightning Source LLC
Chambersburg PA
CBHW060949170426
43202CB00026B/2994